SECRETS
OF AN
EXECUTIVE
COACH

SECRETS
OF AN
EXECUTIVE
COACH

PROVEN METHODS
FOR HELPING LEADERS
EXCEL UNDER PRESSURE

ALAN DOWNS

AMACOM
American Management Association
New York • Atlanta • Brussels • Buenos Aires • Chicago • London • Mexico City
San Francisco • Shanghai • Tokyo • Toronto • Washington, D.C.

Special discounts on bulk quantities of AMACOM books are available to corporations, professional associations, and other organizations. For details, contact Special Sales Department, AMACOM, a division of American Management Association, 1601 Broadway, New York, NY 10019.
Tel.: 212-903-8316. Fax: 212-903-8083.
Web site: www.amacombooks.org

This publication is designed to provide accurate and authoritative information in regard to the subject matter covered. It is sold with the understanding that the publisher is not engaged in rendering legal, accounting, or other professional service. If legal advice or other expert assistance is required, the services of a competent professional person should be sought.

Library of Congress Cataloging-in-Publication Data

Downs, Alan.
    Secrets of an executive coach : proven methods for helping leaders excel under pressure / Alan Downs.
        p. cm.
    Includes index.
    ISBN 0-8144-0697-1 (hardcover)
    1. Executives—Training of. 2. Executive ability. 3. Mentoring in business. 4. Business consultants. I. Title.

HD30.4 .D675 2002
658 .4'0785—dc21

                                                                2002001992

Printing number

10 9 8 7 6 5 4 3 2 1

To those who would have it all:
a career and a dream.

Author's Note

All case studies presented in this book are actual cases of executives who have sought and received coaching. Names, organizations, and the identifying details of the situation have been changed to protect privacy.

All material presented in this book applies equally and without bias to men and women executives. To avoid the semantic awkwardness of simultaneously referring to both genders, I have opted to present the material using the male gender, except when presenting an example that involves a female executive.

CONTENTS

CONTENTS

CONTENTS

PART ONE

THE SECRETS OF COACHING

This first section describes some of the most important practical tips or "secrets" to becoming a successful executive coach. These secrets were gathered from experienced and highly successful coaches when asked to describe the most important lessons they have learned about coaching executives. As such, the information in this section isn't found in any textbook on coaching; rather, it was learned by many professionals who collectively have logged untold hours coaching executives through the toughest situations imaginable.

MAKE IT

PERSONAL

"Don't you understand?" he said as he rubbed his eyes and leaned back into the sumptuous leather chair behind his massive desk. "Repression is the backbone of a corporation."

Staring straight ahead he continued: "Do you really think I give a damn about the millions of dollars in trinkets we sell? Do you think I dreamed this is what my life would amount to? Could I have pulled myself out of bed at the crack of dawn to be here at 7:30 every morning for twenty years if I allowed myself to dwell on it?"

His tone became hushed with the kind of tone that said he was speaking the unutterable truth. "There's hardly a person in this corporate maze of cubicles and conveyors whom I really enjoy or, for that matter, respect. Do you have any idea how many brownnosers sit everyday where you sit trying to say exactly what they think I want to hear? Do you know how many dead-beats and dolts I've had to fire in my career? How many egomaniacs I've had to suffer under? How many deadly cocktail parties I've had to endure? No, the truth is, if I really sat and thought about it, I'd lie down and never get up." Then he added with thoughtful emphasis, "Repression is a wonderful thing."

Those were the words of a struggling CEO. He was brilliant, but floundering to keep a billion-dollar business one step ahead of bankruptcy. On that summer day, long after most everyone else had gone home, he voiced to me what generations of executives now and before him have practiced. You can't let yourself feel too deeply, or you just might not survive the corporate ordeal.

Several years after that conversation, I was saddened to learn that two days after he was fired, he had a massive heart attack and died shortly thereafter.

That day in his office, he spoke of a tragic misconception that so many corporate executives have accepted as truth. Feelings have no place in the corporate world. Corporate life, to him, was an inhumane struggle to survive. If he really allowed himself to feel, he'd never be able to do the work.

This widely held misconception is what created the field of executive coaching. Being a successful executive is more than being brilliant, savvy, tenacious, and forceful. Truly successful executives are *passionate* about their work. They *feel* strongly about what they do, and their inspiration is contagious. They are *energized* by their work. Unless an executive's inner flame or inspiration and passion is lit, he will never realize his potential.

This is the cornerstone truth of executive coaching: The successful executive is both emotionally and mentally fully engaged with his work.

The field of executive coaching has officially been in existence for no more than a decade, although you can be certain it has been practiced ever since the invention of the modern corporation. Coaches by whatever name they call themselves are the detectives of corporate life, peeling away all its façades and games to help executives find the delicate balance of fulfilling their own inner desires while succeeding on the job.

So much of corporate life for many executives is, as that CEO put it, about repression and abdication of one's own desires, values, and sometimes even, convictions. Years of crawling up the corporate ladder teach one to shed the skin of individualism and adopt the persona of perfect corporate citizen. But is this really the way to become a successful executive? Maybe if humans could be mechanical components on a Henry Ford–style assembly line, this would all work out fine. But, of course, we're not that at all.

Executives are endowed with all the greatness of humanity, including passion, values, and dreams. No matter how great the reward or how high the promotion, no executive ever completely abandons these things. He simply pushes them down further inside himself, ignoring if necessary their siren call, to become instead what he thinks will make him successful.

This struggle between the truth of individuality and the demands of corporate life define the domain of the executive coach. Can one successfully deny one's own feelings to become what the corporation needs? Can one follow one's dream and also find success in the corporation?

At the core of this struggle is the ongoing process of *truth management*. Truth management is denying expression to the unique truth of oneself. Executives must practice truth management daily in order to succeed.

You hate your job, but could never say so. Or you have little respect for your boss, but keep that to yourself. Or you know the project you're working on will fail, but you keep at it because your boss thinks differently. Or you conveniently "forget" to respond to that memo from human resources because you know it will only create more paperwork for you.

The unvarnished truth stings, chastens, exhilarates, and infuriates, so we often choose to avoid it. This truth is often connected with powerful feelings that can cause great discomfort and upheaval within careers, so we occupy ourselves instead with managing the truth so it is less cutting and also far less inspiring.

Truth management is a major component of executive failure. It deceivingly promises to minimize pain and maximize success, but—and here's the rub—in the end it only ensnares those who practice it.

The reality is, we all practice truth management and are ensnared by it to a degree. However, the more we rely on it, the further we go from our true selves, creating lives that are stylized, managed, and hollow. When the pressure to manage truth becomes all encompassing, as it does for so many executives, we venture even further into unfulfilling and artificial territory. Then, we wake up one morning at thirty, forty-five, or sixty years of age, and are desperate to discover ourselves again. The managed life we've created suddenly seems suffocatingly wrong and empty. "Who am I?" is the refrain we start to repeat in a thousand different ways.

Imagine how different our lives would be if we were brutally honest about absolutely everything. Everything would change—how we interact with people, our intimate relationships, what projects we work on, and how quickly we advance up the career ladder. There would be no doubt as to who we are, for that would have been our internal compass and unfailing guide.

Sadly, executives must become masters of truth management. They learn the hard way that they must present a certain, acceptable image of themselves and their work if they are to be successful. They learn to gloss over mistakes and trump up successes. They learn to hide conflicts with colleagues behind a mask of false cooperation. In short, they learn to meet the expectations of their powerful superiors, regardless of their own feelings.

Maybe you're thinking, "Can't an executive just act one way at work and be his real self at home?" That's a good question, and the answer may surprise you. No, it really isn't possible to live your life like that. Sure, you might be able to do it for a month or even a few years, but slowly your grasp on your own values and feelings will begin to slip. The values and feelings are still there; it's just that your familiarity in experiencing them becomes vague and less certain. The question, "What do I feel about my situation?" becomes "What *should* I feel about this situation?" Rather than working through your own process of discovering your feelings, you abandon that and immediately drift to what you are expected to feel.

In real life, truth management works just fine until the day comes when you find yourself unable to manage some uncomfortable and strong feelings. Dissatisfaction, frustration, anger, disappointment, and unhappiness well up inside you and refuse to be managed. These feelings begin to spill out in a myriad of behaviors and in subtly veiled translations. The more you try to manage those feelings, the deeper you find yourself mired in their control.

So you turn much of your attention and energy to suppressing and repressing these unacceptable and unmanageable feelings. You find yourself and your career slowed by the constant need to deny and silence these feelings. Eventually, something traumatic happens, and it all comes spilling out. Now, you're in real trouble.

This is the arena of an executive in crisis who is consumed by frustration and disappointment, and is the best opportunity for the executive coach. This is where the coach can do his best work.

In a corporate world where truth management reigns, the executive coach must enter as the champion of truth. The coach is uniquely equipped to cut through the denial and superficial platitudes, to get to the real issue at the core of an executive's troubled career: the truth about what the executive feels about his life, job, relationships, and future.

Secret #1: Create a safe space for dangerous feelings, and those feelings will always lead you to the source of the problem and its solution.

Of all the trade secrets we'll explore, this one is by far the most important and best kept from those outside the field. The coach is nothing less than a bounty hunter of repressed feelings within the executive. He, in essence, helps the executive to put aside truth management for a while and rediscover his own process of feelings, values, and dreams.

No one else in the corporation is prepared to unleash the power of these feelings. For most people, it is uncomfortable and even unseemly to talk about such things, but not for the coach. The coach knows that it is the management of truth that creates the quicksand in which the troubled executive is sinking. The only real and lasting solution is to arrest all the tactics of truth management and thereby firm the ground on which the executive's career lies. The coach, more than anyone else at work today, knows that *feelings are important business.* Furthermore, the coach knows that there is no line between an executive's business and personal life. Everything about being a successful executive is personal.

As an executive, you may hire someone whom you wouldn't choose as a friend, but you'd never promote someone you didn't trust. You may successfully work with someone you intensely dislike, but you'd never voluntarily partner with him on your career-making project. You may even work for a jerk, but you won't excel under him.

The bottom line is that there is no barrier between your personal world of feelings, ideas, and motivations and your business world. How you feel, think, and act about work is deeply personal. The business decisions you make, the risks you agree to bear, and the job you take are all very personal.

Sure, you may create the illusion that part of your life is "business" and the rest is "personal," but when push comes to shove, you'll always make the important business decisions in your personal way. Where you work, where you live, how hard you work, and with whom you do your most productive work will ultimately be intertwined with your inner feelings.

What differentiates an excellent executive from all the others? He *wants* to be where he is. He is truly present and genuinely *excited* about his work. He *cares* about the company and its success. He is deeply *involved* with his work, the organization, and his career. He comes across as authentic and personable with others.

What do all these things have in common? They are based on feelings. Strong feelings like desire, dreams, passion, and excitement are the dynamo behind the heroes—the ones who reach higher and go further. Excellence requires skill, but skill isn't sufficient for excellence. You have to be emotionally engaged to excel.

When you look down the corridors of corporate history, you see the walls of honor decorated with photographs of executives who were above all *passionate* about their work.

- ❖ J. Paul Getty once wrote of the ideal businessman, "[H]e must be a creative artist rather than merely an artisan of business."

- ❖ Willard Rockwell, founder of Rockwell International Corp., said of the unfeeling executive, "He will be limited in generating the warmth and rapport that are so essential to the development of trusting relationships at high levels and the consummation of important business deals."

- ❖ Mary Kay Ash, founder of Mary Kay Cosmetics, was often heard to say that the only thing she founded her company with was enthusiasm.

- ❖ Sam Walton, founder of Wal-Mart Stores Inc., was notorious for turning company meetings into pep rallies.

- ❖ Bill Gates, founder of Microsoft Corp., was known to be so involved in his work that he wouldn't leave the office for days at a time.

If you pry off the façade of machismo and business school rhetoric, it's clear that the one secret to business success is drive and passion. It's all about emotional engagement.

That's why the executive coach is so concerned about feelings. If an executive is failing, nine times out of ten it is because he isn't emotionally involved and committed to his job, organization, and career. The coach has the job of helping the executive sweep away the layers of denial to rediscover what really turns him on. Only when an executive is tuned into his feelings, and following that passion with all his heart, will he find the will and tenacity to succeed, both professionally and personally. An executive who isn't emotionally involved with his work is simply a placeholder in the organization.

It's not about what the executive *should* feel, or about what he feels might get him ahead. It's about what really turns him on, rocks his boat, and gets him out of bed in the morning singing. It's about tremulous excitement with success and tears with failure. It's about following a dream.

Sadly, many executives have abandoned their dreams and passion to adopt the "look" of emotional engagement with their work. They work long hours. They learn all the buzz phrases in the trade journals. They never take all their earned vacation and very rarely call in sick. They don't drive a more expensive car than the CEO, even when they can afford it.

But conformity to corporate norms is no substitute for emotional engagement. In his book of business advice, *How to Be Rich*, J. Paul Getty wrote about the businessman who is snared by the pitfall of conformity: "He'll conform to petty, arbitrary codes and convention desperately trying to prove himself stable and reliable—but he will only demonstrate that he is unimaginative, unenterprising, and mediocre."

Helping executives rediscover emotional engagement with their work is the cornerstone and calling of the executive coach. Every successful executive coach has this mantra clearly in mind at all times: If it isn't personally relevant, it *isn't* relevant.

Secret #2: The executive who believes his business decisions have nothing to do with his personal feelings is engaging in the defense mechanism of disassociation.

Disassociative defenses abound in the business world. Everywhere employees, supervisors, and executives try to segment their lives, separating out certain parts as "just business" and "not me." As an executive coach, don't fall prey to this defense. No one (that's right, not even one person) can operate at his highest level of effectiveness when he is splitting himself into parts.

Let me explain this in more depth. You are a whole person—what psychologists call a *Gestalt*. You are not merely the sum of your various roles in life: father, executive, husband, friend, and son. You move through your day without a break in consciousness and your experience of yourself remains the same no matter which of your roles you are engaging. Simply, you are *you*.

You are a whole person, and in each role you play, you must engage that whole person to be truly effective. For example, you must use all your life experiences with risky decisions when you are called upon to make a high-risk decision at work. If you make that decision strictly on the business facts in front of you, you're likely to make a less than optimal decision. You know a great deal about risk from your life experiences: what it is, how to manage it, and how much of it you can tolerate. When you try to segment your life by making an "objective" business decision, you're fooling yourself.

Psychologists have long known that nothing is truly objective. Everything is perceived through your senses and processed by a brain that is biased by your lifetime of experiences. It is a myth that anything in life, particularly in business, is objective. Everything is subjective, biased, laced with personal feelings, and driven by personalities.

So when an executive insists that personal issues have no relevance to work, he is trying to disown something about himself. The defense mechanism of disassociation is a big clue to the experienced executive coach. What is it that the client wants to disown? What part of himself is he uncomfortable with? Why does he want to split off part of himself from his work?

When the successful executive coach sees a client, he doesn't see just an executive. He sees a whole person, with no walls dividing that person's experience of himself. He refuses to limit inquiry into just the "business" aspects of his life, for he knows that everything about him must be engaged in order for the executive to be successful. An executive is a person, not a corporate machine that operates from nine to five. Everything about that person is grist for the coach and client to consider.

The executive in need of coaching doesn't need a new model of project management or a new set of people skills; he is in deep trouble and needs help—and that's what a coach has to offer. The coach helps the executive cut through the layers of denial and suppression to discover exactly where he went off course.

Secret #3: In almost all cases, executives become executives because they have the requisite skills to do the job.

Sure, an executive may lack a certain something in the business skill set, but you can trust that he has what it takes to succeed. You don't rise to the executive level by being overly deficient in management skills. Unless something is terribly wrong with the organization, you rise because you have most of the necessary potential. Maybe back in the days of the "organization man" you could rise to the executive ranks on tenure alone, but I don't know an organization around today where that is still true—and I'll bet you don't either.

Furthermore, most executives are promoted into increasingly higher levels of management because they have created some past successes. Somewhere, somehow, they were able to do something good that eluded others. They stood out and achieved results.

Secret #4: When a previously successful executive starts to fail, something in his life is interfering with his potential.

Your job is to help the executive discover the "something" that is interfering and blocking him from success, and then help him *resolve* it.

The "something" of executive coaching is what I call a *crisis*—an inner situation of conflict between what an executive wants in life and what the executive is actually experiencing. We'll come back to this definition often, and it will become a premise of our executive coaching model. As an executive coach, you will always be on the hunt for the crisis at the root of the problem.

Secret #5: An executive is in crisis only when he feels he is in crisis.

Crisis is not defined by a corporation or a boss. There is no crisis until the executive feels strong dissonance within, regardless of what others might think of his performance. For example, if my boss doesn't like the numbers I've achieved, but I am truly satisfied with my results, there is no crisis. I may not remain employed, but I'm not in crisis. Furthermore, executive coaching does little good in this situation.

On the other hand, I am in crisis when the numbers I achieve are less than the numbers I desire and, despite my best efforts, I can't improve them. That is a true crisis, and is fertile ground for a skilled executive coach.

Crisis is an inner state, not an external judgment about an executive's performance. Until there is a crisis, there is little an executive coach can do.

Secret #6: Executive coaching is most effective with an executive who is experiencing a crisis.

This is extremely important, and I want you to remember this carefully, because it will save you a great deal of heartache as an executive coach: You can't help an executive who doesn't admit that he is in crisis. Why? Because he's not in crisis until he feels he is in crisis—and until that happens, even the best executive coaches are of little use.

In the rush to sell their services and build a clientele, some inexperienced executive coaches have attempted to broaden their appeal with claims that they can help any executive. Sadly, they try to offer all the warmed-over business models that corporate trainers have taught for years. My experience is that this just isn't helpful—or cost effective. A coach can offer advice, helpful recommendations, and new ideas, but the effect of the coaching is minimal unless the executive has reached a dead end on his own, and is ready to own responsibility for the problem. Given the expense of hiring an executive coach, the only solid return on investment is coaching for those executives who are clearly experiencing a crisis.

Not every executive who is failing is in a crisis. Furthermore, most executives will experience crises only at critical points in their careers. The point is this: There is an optimal time in an executive's career when he is experiencing crisis and when coaching is immensely helpful. The successful executive coach knows this and only takes clients who are ready to benefit from the services he offers. The coach isn't a cheerleader, a corporate handyman, or a superexecutive. He has a specific skill and trade: helping executives to successfully navigate their crises. When the coach tries to be all things to all clients, he only determines his own failure. I learned this lesson the hard way. Learn from my experience: You can't fix everything for your clients. You can only help a client with a problem that he experiences and accepts responsibility for.

This brings us to the first step in successful executive coaching: owning the crisis. In the next chapter, we'll explore this important first step in greater depth.

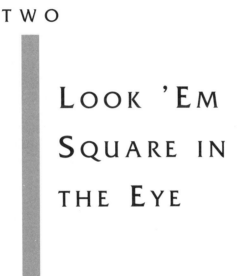

TWO

LOOK 'EM SQUARE IN THE EYE

Secret #7: An executive must first take responsibility for experiencing a crisis before he can begin to work on resolving the crisis.

Taking responsibility for a crisis is the first and most difficult step toward crisis resolution and success. A person can't fix what he doesn't acknowledge is broken.

"I have a problem." "I need help." "I am in trouble." These are the phrases that acknowledge a crisis, and they are extremely important. Perhaps this may seem obvious, but you'd surprised how many clients come to coaching with an unwillingness to acknowledge that they are in trouble. They will say things like: "My boss thought this might be good for me," or "There's no problem, I just want to improve myself," or "Every other executive in the company has a coach, so I thought I should have one, too."

As an executive coach, your first task from the minute you meet your new client is to get to ownership. The client must be ready to say: "There is a problem here, and *I am responsible*."

In my experience and in the experience of many executive coaches I know, an executive seeking "general personal improvement" doesn't really benefit from coaching and, in fact, can actually be disserved by it. In this latter case, a few executives attempt to use their coach as a crutch for decision making by relying heavily on the coach to tell them what to do. While this kind of coaching arrangement can generate a good deal of business for the coach, it doesn't help the executive improve and is considered unethical.

Another reason coaching for general personal improvement usually doesn't benefit the executive is because without a crisis, there isn't a strong motive to learn—a critical element in any learning situation. For example, if you've ever taken a computer class, you know that unless you have a pressing need to use the information at the time you are taught it, much of the information doesn't stay with you. Why? Because you didn't have a strong motive to learn and practice what you were taught. The same is true in the coaching relationship: Unless there is some present difficulty in the executive's career, there isn't likely to be much learning.

Often executives who are quietly struggling with a crisis will present themselves for coaching for general personal improvement. These executives can actually benefit from coaching if they are willing to acknowledge the crisis they are experiencing. The coach, in this situation, needs to push the executive a little further to see if there is a crisis and if the executive is willing to acknowledge it. Sometimes, all an executive needs is for you to give him permission to call a crisis a "crisis."

Creating a situation where an executive takes ownership isn't for the weakhearted executive coach. It isn't for the people-pleasers or those who want to build their coaching career by not offending an executive. It takes guts and persistence, because executives are extremely adept at avoiding responsibility for problems. Remember our discussion of truth management? A big part of it is learning how to pin problems on something or someone else.

Executives learn to win the corporate game by claiming their victories and distancing themselves from defeats. They learn to externalize the problem, carefully blame it on competitors, customers, other departments, you name it . . . the list is long. Executives are generally great salespeople, and if you don't stick to your guns, your client might just sell you a bill of goods.

Secret #8: Never allow your client to become a victim.

You'll hear it all—all of the things the client blames his problem on. Bad customers. Lazy employees. Late suppliers. No support from upper management. Downturn in the economy.

Is any of this true? Maybe some of it. Maybe even most of it. But the way in which you will help this executive is not by focusing on what others are or are not doing, but by forcing the executive to take a hard look at himself and own the situation, including he how he feels about it. That's the pipeline of real insight and transformation.

You've got to stick your guns and be unrelenting in your focus on ownership. "How have you created this situation?" "What could you have done differently here?" "What can you do to improve it now?" These are important questions you need to ask in a dozen different ways until you and your client are clear that the client is responsible for what has happened.

CASE STUDY

IT ISN'T JERRY'S PROBLEM

Jerry was a hard-driving executive at a leading stock brokerage firm. He had personally been responsible for adding over $100 million to the firm's portfolio and his financial wizardry was unmatched. Jerry was brilliant and, according to just about everyone else in his office, a jerk. Arrogant, always right and never-to-be-questioned, demanding, and yes, extremely good at making winning financial decisions.

Jerry's firm thought he might benefit from coaching. Perhaps the coach could help him soften his approach and help him become a bit easier to be around.

According to Jerry, he had made more money for the firm than anyone else in the office, or for that matter, in the whole region. He saw himself as a broker's broker, and he didn't have time for all the office politics that everyone else thought was so important. If they'd just learn to focus on the market and stop all the nonsense, they might be as successful as he was, or so he asserted.

Jerry wasn't a good candidate for coaching. He didn't own his portion of the problem and saw no reason to change. In fact, he saw the problem as everyone else's but his. Furthermore, Jerry was deeply involved in disassociating his "personal" and "business" lives. He didn't see any reason why personal issues of how one related to other people should have any relevance to his performance or potential for promotion. He was good at making money with the stock market. What else mattered?

Not until Jerry understands his crisis will he be ready for coaching. Perhaps it will be a sudden streak of bad financial decisions or being passed over for a coveted promotion that will trigger his crisis. Until that happens, there's not much a coach can offer Jerry.

CASE STUDY

BETSY'S DILEMMA

When I first met Betsy in the visitors' lobby of the high-tech firm where she worked, she appeared to me to be the image of success. Confident, charming, well dressed, and as I learned from her office walls, very well educated. What more could she need?

Quickly I found out. It wasn't more than a minute after she shut the door to her office that her in-charge façade slid right on to the floor. As she poured out her troubles, it was clear that Betsy was in deep crisis.

Early in her career Betsy had been very successful and was promoted quickly through the ranks of human resources. After she completed a prestigious MBA in marketing, she rose rapidly through the marketing department. She had had a string of hits, such as an award-winning television commercial series that had not only caught the eye of consumers, but industry watchers and investors as well. She and her staff had completely transformed the image of her company as a rather stodgy, old engineering firm into a hip and cutting-edge computer outfit. Sales had skyrocketed and business couldn't have been better. Betsy was now the senior executive vice president of marketing.

But Betsy didn't want to get out of bed in the morning. She struggled to keep her mind on her work and avoided returning phone messages and e-mails for days. She was coasting on her past successes, and she knew it. The problem was, she didn't have the interest or the energy to dream up anything new.

In our work together, it became clear that Betsy was highly creative and loved anything artistic. She had worked in the editing room, literally piecing together video segments for those fantastic commercials—and she had loved every minute of it. But once that project was over and the day-today grind of managing a 200-employee department settled on her shoulders, she slowly sank under the drudgery. There wasn't anything creative about her job now, and she had grown to despise it. But what could she do? Everyone thought she was a marketing whiz. All she could think about was opening a small advertising firm of her own. Maybe, just maybe, that would let her spend her days doing what she really enjoyed doing.

The important point here is to recognize that Betsy was a prime candidate to benefit from coaching. She was in a crisis and owned it completely. She had tried to correct the situation, but couldn't and was clearly ready for help. Betsy, and clients like her, are dream clients.

Not all clients will be as eager and open as Betsy. The challenge is for you as an executive coach to ferret out those clients who are ready and those who are not. Some clients will immediately own the problem, while others won't do so at first, but will with minimal work. Other clients won't own the problem at all.

This latter client often breaks appointments with you, appears to give your work together a low priority, and from session to session, doesn't seem to remember much of what happened in the previous session. This client will usually complain about the cost of coaching and the lack of clear, deliverable objectives. "I'm not seeing how this is relevant?" he'll say. "Why are we wasting time on this?" he'll ask.

Secret #9: The client, not the coach, does the work.

You will be tempted—every executive coach is from time to time—to try and win over this client by setting objectives and making your sessions with the client seem productive. You may try numerous exercises, lots of reading materials, 360-degree surveys, customer feedback—you name it—but it won't work.

Why? Because the client does the work in coaching, not you. You are there to facilitate and guide, but not to set the agenda. The client must take responsibility for the work if real change is to happen.

Think of it this way. What does a sports coach do? He pushes the athletes to work harder and smarter. He helps the athlete find motivation within himself to go further and to be better. The coach doesn't supply the motivation or the skill; he simply helps the athlete find more of both within himself.

If the client tells you he doesn't see any value in coaching, agree with him that coaching probably isn't right for him and walk away from the job. Don't let your personal issues of achievement and pride steer you wrong. It isn't up to you to *make* coaching happen; all you do is show up and supply your knowledge of how to resolve crises. The client does the real work.

When you are faced with an unwilling client, the most responsible choice you can make for yourself and your client is to terminate the work. If you don't, very little good will result, and eventually it will reflect badly on you, no matter how much effort you pour into the work. Learning to select clients who are likely to succeed under coaching is as important as the coaching itself. You can never underestimate the importance of client readiness to the success of the coaching process.

Secret #10: Keep a clear focus at all times on how the client feels.

Once you've established that client does own the problem, your job is to push further into muddy waters.

"How do you feel about the situation?" "Are you disappointed in yourself?" "Do you feel frustrated or angry?" "When was the last time you really felt excitement about your work?"

Does this line of inquiry make you squirm? It shouldn't, at least not once you've started work as an executive coach. And why is it necessary? You're hunting for the crisis at the root of this client's problem, and these types of questions often elicit the most important clues you can find. Remember the first and most important trade secret of executive coaching: *Create a safe space for dangerous feelings, and those feelings will always lead you to the source of the problem and its solution.*

Feelings and business have had a long and tumultuous marriage. Business denies that feelings even exist, while feelings seem at odds with strategy and good decision making. What does it matter to you how an executive "feels" as long as he is doing the job?

I suppose from a strictly managerial point of view, you might not care how someone feels about himself and his work. Certainly, decades of MBA graduates have been taught not to care, or that caring is somehow soft and weak.

Of course, this attitude is precisely what has created the need for executive coaches. No amount of pretending feelings don't exist will make them go away.

Secret #11: An executive coach should never attempt to play the role of the executive's manager.

Always keep this trade secret in mind: *The coach is not the client's manager.* You are there to help your client reach his highest potential, not to direct his work. An effective coach never makes decisions for a client or tells a client what to do on the job.

This is a fine line that always must be observed. Crossing the line not only interferes with the organizational structure, it can build a dependency upon the coach rather than help the client to deal with his own crisis. Whenever the client asks you what he should do, a good response is, "What do you think you should do?"

Secret #12: The role and purpose of the executive coach is very different from that of a management consultant or human resources representative.

The unique value of the executive coach is your concern about feelings. No one else on the job or in the company is really concerned about his feelings. That's your role, and the more skilled you become at creating a safe relationship with the client where he can freely explore and express his feelings, the more successful you will be.

Those feelings that everyone else is so uncomfortable talking about are your primary tool of transformation. Your ability to ferret out those feelings and help the client interpret the clues they offer is what differentiates you from all the other host of consultants and management gurus who offer help.

The role of executive coach is best suited for an expert who is an external contractor; although, with certain safeguards, coaching can be effectively done by an internal employee. Whether the coach is internal or external, all information provided by the client should be strictly confidential and kept completely separate from any decisions regarding the executive's employment.

Secret #13: An executive who is inspired will outperform an executive who isn't—every time.

When a client feels excited, inspired, motivated, and good about his job, it makes all the difference in the world. You can take an executive with mediocre business skills who feels great about what he is doing and then compare him with another executive who has excellent business skills who doesn't feel good about his job, and the mediocre executive will exceed and excel every time. This is true so often that it is practically a law of business.

Likewise, when an executive is in trouble, it almost always has something to do with how he feels about his job and/or his life. You will help him clarify those feelings and create a plan whereby he can begin to feel better about what he is doing. Your end goal is to have an executive who feels inspired and motivated. That executive, regardless of his skill set, will find a way to succeed.

Feelings affect the executive's job in two important areas: motivation and relationships. As we begin to look at the specific crises that an executive might experience, we will look at the two general categories, motivational crises and relationship crises. One or both is almost always at the bottom of the executive's difficulty, and resolving that crisis is ultimately the source of the solution. Your job as an executive coach is to create a situation where the client feels safe enough to see this for himself—not because you tell him, but because he has the insight and tells you. Once the client is at this point, you're well on your way to helping him bring about real transformation in his career.

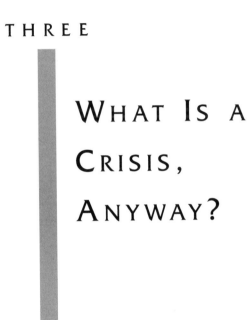

THREE

WHAT IS A CRISIS, ANYWAY?

Everyone experiences crises, not just executives. Throughout your life, you have experienced and will experience crises. At one point or another, you'll struggle with the meaning of your life, finding your passion, overcoming the demons of your past, and surviving broken dreams. It's just a fact of life.

A crisis isn't life-threatening, but it is painful, and if it continues, it can be debilitating. When you're in the middle of a crisis, there's no place more miserable.

A crisis is when you experience a painful void in your life between what you want and what you are experiencing. You've done everything you know, and still, you wind up at the same place, with the same results you swore you wouldn't repeat again. So here you are, right back where you never wanted to be.

High-ranking executives, ministers, therapists, and Pulitzer prize–winning authors all have crises. Smart people, rich people, happily married people, single people, old people, young people all experience crisis. It's easy to think that smart or successful people have no crises in their lives, but that is dead wrong. Money, intelligence, power, and success are no insurance against crisis, and in fact, often make crises worse. *Everyone* experiences the crises of living.

All executives experience crisis at one point or another in their careers, too. Just because they appear successful, powerful, organized, and assertive doesn't make them one bit more immune to the experience of crisis than anyone else. In fact, all of those things often compound to make the executive's crisis all the more acute and painful.

As we've already seen, the job of the executive coach is to help his client navigate the crises that are affecting his career. These crises are remarkably similar to the crises everyone else experiences; however, there are a few very significant ways in which each crisis differs. Further, there are a handful of crises that are quite common among troubled executives. In the remaining chapters of this book, we'll examine closely these executive crises and the unique way an executive experiences each crisis.

Secret #14: A crisis first appears in the executive's life as a "latent crisis."

There are four ways in which each crisis can manifest in an executive's life. It can be a:

❖ Latent crisis

❖ Inflamed crisis

❖ Suppressed crisis

❖ Resolved crisis

To begin with, a crisis first appears in the executive's life as a latent crisis. That is, it is present but not causing him any pain. For example, he may be aware that he really isn't inspired by his work, but doesn't have the driving need to make a job change. In this case, his crisis of passion is a latent crisis.

If, however, his best friend dies suddenly of a heart attack at the office, he may find himself wondering what it is all about and longing to find work that is more than just a paycheck and an occasional promotion. Suddenly, his latent crisis has become inflamed. He's in pain and needs some solid answers. An inflamed crisis is the most painful and most distressing form of crisis.

Secret #15: A triggering event turns a latent crisis into an inflamed crisis.

What makes a latent crisis become an inflamed crisis? Almost always it is a painful or traumatic event that activates the latent crisis and starts the cycle of frustration and pain. An important project fails. The marriage falls apart. A disabling heart attack forces a career change. A child fails in school. The long-awaited promotion is given to someone else.

Whatever the event might be, it unleashes the energy of the latent crisis, and the executive begins to experience great distress. It's more than just the pain of a broken relationship or a lost job—the executive begins to have some serious and painful questions about life. The questions keep him up at night and hound him during the day. There's no escape from his crisis that has become inflamed.

The executive first *experiences* a crisis when it becomes inflamed. When the crisis is latent, it isn't experienced as a crisis—in fact, the executive may not be aware of it at all. It takes a triggering event to bring a latent crisis into full awareness and make it inflamed.

Once inflamed, an executive has two choices: He can either suppress the crisis (for example, by taking on more work to distract himself from the feeling that he isn't fulfilled by his work) or he can resolve his crisis—a process that the executive coach can help facilitate.

Secret #16: Suppressing a crisis keeps the executive locked into a repeating behavioral pattern.

When an executive is locked into a repeating pattern that he just can't seem to break, it happens for one reason: He's suppressing a crisis rather than resolving it. A suppressed crisis is when he experiences a crisis and, rather than confront and resolve it, he pushes it back into the recesses of his mind in an effort to avoid the pain it is causing. There are many ways he might suppress a crisis. For example, he might distract himself with busyness, or medicate himself with an addictive substance, or throw himself into a mind-numbing depression.

However he does it, suppressing a crisis has one monumental negative side effect: It keeps the executive stuck in the same repeating circumstances. Because he's acting out of fear and avoidance, he can't move forward and instead remains in the same painful circumstances.

Suppressing a crisis takes lots of energy. It slowly depletes the executive's internal resources, leaving him unable to grow, take risks, and move forward with his career.

Secret #17: Every executive has latent crises that have not yet been inflamed.

There are a couple of important points you should remember about executive crises. First, every executive has latent crises. These are conflicts that are beneath the surface and really aren't experienced as painful or conflicting. Given the right event, however, these crises can spring to full life, creating havoc in the executive's life and career. A crisis can exist as a latent crisis for years before it ever becomes inflamed.

Perhaps it seems a bit odd to you to think of executives as walking time bombs that could blow at any moment. Well, it isn't exactly like that. It is simply that they are human beings, like everyone else, with hidden vulnerabilities. Given the right set of circumstances or unfortunate twists of fate, these vulnerabilities become exposed and problematic. Once exposed, or "inflamed," they must be resolved if the executive is to move forward in his career.

Secret #18: At first, suppressing a crisis appears to be easier than resolving it.

This brings us to the second point you need to remember. Executives often try to suppress their crises rather than resolve them. A crisis can be so overwhelming that it threatens to destroy everything one has worked so hard in life to achieve and, as a result, it is avoided or "suppressed."

In this case, the executive takes energy away from his creative side and applies it to suppressing the crisis and avoiding pain. He distracts himself with more work, bigger challenges, or exotic vacations. That works fine until something else happens to inflame the suppressed crisis that lurks just beneath the surface. Then, the executive blows up at his boss and quits on the spot. Or he tells off that unpleasant client who gives him millions of dollars in business. Or the executive fires an otherwise excellent employee because he challenged him on his most vulnerable area.

Of course, this is a type of emotional engagement with one's work, but it is the kind of emotional engagement that occurs after years of frustration and denial of one's feelings. It's like an eruption of emotion that can no longer be contained. It is unfocused and destructive in nature.

The job of the executive coach is to help the executive resolve this crisis quickly once it becomes inflamed and before it does serious damage to his career. This is a far cry from the conventional corporate responses that are generally aimed at helping the executive to suppress the crisis, rather than resolve it. These "conventional responses" include statements such as: "Take a good, long vacation and get yourself back together." "Maybe what you need is change of scenery. What do you think about taking the position down in Florida?" "I don't know what's going on with you, but you better pull yourself together before you lose everything you've worked for around here." Or my all time favorite, "Maybe you need a little more attention than you're getting at home these days."

Even more enlightened management training programs participate in the executive's suppressive and dissociative defense by treating the problem strictly as a management skill problem rather than as a crisis that has emotional roots. These programs advocate techniques such as "managing personal growth" and "strategic personal plans" that try to objectify and de-emotionalize the issue.

Secret #19: The executive coach insists that the executive focus on resolving the crisis rather than suppressing it.

Your job is not to help the executive suppress the crisis, but to resolve it. You can't allow the executive's crisis to magically disappear into the fog of denial; you've got to keep it alive until he deals with it squarely.

What? Keep the crisis alive? That's right, you help keep it alive. You see, suppression is a very strong and powerful temptation, not a solution. It will make the crisis magically disappear over the short term, but the crisis will always come roaring back.

Your best way to help an executive in crisis is to force him to work on the crisis that he is experiencing. When he tries to avoid, blame, shame, excuse, or depress the crisis away, you refuse to allow it. You keep reminding him of the issues and keep the focus on resolution of those issues.

Remember what I said about this not being work for people-pleasers? I think you're starting to see what I mean by that now. Sometimes your strongest tool is confrontation and persistence in the face of a powerful executive who would rather sweep issues under the rug than deal with them. One thing is for sure: It isn't easy.

However, if you're willing to hang in there, the rewards of executive coaching can be enormous. When the light starts to dawn and your client begins to turn the corner toward success, you'll both be glad you kept a steady focus on the crisis at hand.

So far we've been talking about crises in a somewhat abstract form, and this may leave you a bit confused. Don't worry, the majority of this book is dedicated to talking about specific crises, how to diagnose them, and the steps that will bring about resolution. For now, you need to understand the overall experience of crisis in the executive's life. The specifics will come later.

Secret #20: It is very easy to confuse the triggering event with the underlying crisis that it inflames.

There's a point that's critical to know. It is easy to confuse the event that triggers a crisis with the crisis itself. What this means is that the event that throws an executive into full-blown crisis isn't the problem. The failed product line isn't the problem. The divorce isn't the problem. The blowup in front of the important customer isn't the problem. The affair with the employee isn't the problem.

The problem is much deeper. As a new executive coach, I often confused the triggering event with the crisis and it caused me great difficulty. I hope you can learn from my mistakes. The event that triggers the crisis is only a catalyst, not the cause.

A common mistake made in coaching executives is to focus on the triggering event. We focus on the situation that went wrong and try to fix it. Our typical solutions to these events are to recommend training in any number of areas, including time management or dealing with difficult people. While these kinds of training can be helpful, they are designed specifically to address situational behaviors, not inner conflicts. To the executive in crisis they're often like putting a Band-Aid on a mortal wound—it just won't work.

That's why, if you've ever attended or even taught these programs (and I've taught lots of them over the years), you've noticed the inevitable cynicism that fills the training room. Somehow we all know that what is being taught is well and good, but it won't solve the kinds of problems that we often see. There's something deeper going on, and the resistance of the training program and trainer to deal with it can be frustrating and, for some, even angering.

When your boss is a tyrant, no amount of "managing upward" is going to save the day. Or when your employee is consistently "out to lunch," performance management is more likely to make you both frustrated than to really change behavior. What is likely is that both the tyrannical boss and the apathetic employee are caught in the grips of a suppressed crisis that is consuming their energy and draining their motivation. Until they deal with these crises, the results, regardless of the "management program," are likely to be the same.

The temptation to focus on the triggering event, to even get down into minute post hoc analysis of the details, is more about suppression than it is about resolution. If I can keep the focus on the situation, and not on me, then I can distract myself (and the executive coach) away from the real crisis that is far too threatening to face.

Don't be fooled. The problem situation is only a symptom—and treating symptoms never leads to a lasting cure. You've got to stay focused on the real problem if you want to be of real and lasting help to your executive client.

Secret #21: The end goal of all coaching is to increase the executive's emotional engagement with his work.

The process of coaching an executive who is experiencing a crisis can best be described as *facilitating* the executive's emotional engagement with his work.

To understand this concept more fully, let's take a quick look at the job of sports coaches. What do they do? Sports coaches generally perform two important tasks:

1. Determine strategy

2. Build enthusiasm, inspiration, and commitment (emotional engagement) with the game

The executive coach, however, has a slightly different job. Whereas the athlete follows the strategy set by the coach, it is the executive's job to determine strategy in conjunction with superiors and the larger organizational objectives. Executives who seek coaching often do so because they have difficulty setting strategy. The fastest help you could give this executive would be to help him with strategy suggestions. You could provide examples of strategies that other organizations and executives have used. Or you could provide textbook models of how to determine and execute strategy. Perhaps you could even become a shadow consultant who feeds the executive strategy ideas from behind the scenes.

I'm convinced, however, that these often-practiced approaches to coaching are deeply flawed. Why? Because they fail to address the more important question of why this executive has become blocked and unable to set an effective management strategy on his own. In other words, the executive coach doesn't provide his client with business strategies—he helps the client overcome the block that has prevented him from discovering those strategies for himself.

To help you understand the difference I'm underscoring here, take a good look around you at all the executives you know who are successful. Are all of them brilliant strategists? For that matter, are all of them brilliant? I'll bet not. Yet they are successful. Maybe they've just had a long run of good luck. I don't think that's plausible, either. If you'll look closely at those successful executives, you'll discover that what drives them is a burning and compelling concern for their work.

The truth is that an executive doesn't have to be a brilliant strategist. He just has to be committed to his work and motivated enough to discover a brilliant strategy. Today there are business books on strategy by the hundreds published every year. In every industry and every profession there are numerous conferences that discuss current strategies in depth. On top of this, there are business strategy consulting firms operating in virtually every country and major city on this planet. If an executive needs to discover an effective strategy, his options are numerous.

I've worked with computer executives who couldn't write a line of computer code or design a piece of hardware to save their souls, but they were highly successful. I've worked with more than a few retail executives who have never worked in a store in their entire lives, yet they are brilliant at marketing merchandise in their stores. I've even worked with advertising executives who couldn't tell you the difference between a flathead and a Philips head screwdriver, but have designed an award-winning advertising campaign that made their chain of hardware stores one of the largest in the country.

The important point to remember here is that executives don't fail because they lack the ability to "think strategically"—executives fail because they aren't engaged enough with the work to be strategic about it.

For example, if you've always wanted to visit Disney World with your family and the opportunity finally arrives for you to do so, you will most likely research everything about Disney World and the surrounding area so that you don't miss anything. You think about the possibility of rain and think about how you can be prepared if it does rain. You think about hotels, rental cars, and the amount of money you'll need to do everything you'd like to do. Even if you're not a great trip planner, you will be strategic about your trip to Disney World so that you and your family will get the most out of it.

When you are emotionally involved with something, you spend time thinking about it and planning for it. You care about the outcome and you want to plan for every contingency. While a trip to Disney World may be infinitely simpler than running a large corporation, the principle of the matter remains the same. When an executive is emotionally engaged in his work, he will find a way to be strategic about it.

So what is it that causes an executive to be disengaged emotionally from his work? Something happens that siphons off his emotional energy. Somehow his inspiration and heartfelt motivation is distracted. His attention is focused not on the content of his work, but on something else that is impinging upon his life.

Of course, the "something" that I'm referring to is what we've already seen is a crisis. When a crisis becomes inflamed, it reaches the point of almost totally consuming an executive's emotional focus, leaving very little for his work. Each crisis has its own unique way of consuming an executive's emotional energy.

Parts Three and Four of this book examine six types of crisis that can block an executive's emotional engagement with his work. Briefly, here are the six crises:

- ❖ *Crisis of Individuation.* The executive becomes obsessed with being part of the team or power structure of the organization.

- ❖ *Crisis of Inferiority.* The executive becomes obsessed with disproving his own feeling of inferiority by being superior to those with whom he works.

- ❖ *Crisis of Isolation.* The executive becomes obsessed with the shortcomings of others and consequently focuses his energy on withdrawing, blaming others, and becoming completely self-sufficient.

- ❖ *Crisis of Passion.* The executive becomes overwhelmed with a sense of meaninglessness and lack of inspiration.

- ❖ *Crisis of Broken Dreams.* The executive becomes consumed with feelings of disappointment, discouragement, and even cynicism over past failures and missed expectations.

- ❖ *Crisis of Self-Confidence.* The executive obsesses on his own shortcomings and concentrates on avoiding failure at all costs.

In each crisis, the executive is no longer able to direct the full force of his energy toward his work, but is sidetracked into pouring most of his attention onto the painful issues of his crisis. As long as the executive is unable to resolve the crisis, he cannot be emotionally engaged with his work.

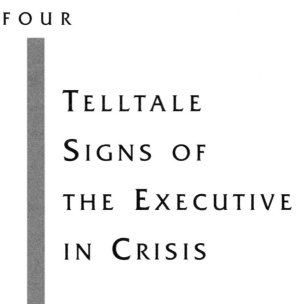

FOUR

TELLTALE SIGNS OF THE EXECUTIVE IN CRISIS

The signs of an executive who is caught in a crisis are clear, once you learn to recognize them. Each crisis does have its own peculiar symptoms, but there are certain symptoms that are across-the-board signs of an executive in crisis. When you see them in a client, you can be immediately certain that coaching can be of help.

Choking

In athletics, as well as in the workplace, some people perform below their proven ability when the pressure is high. They become tense and self-conscious, almost as if they are deliberately trying to sabotage their own success. The term for this kind of self-sabotage is *choking*, and it refers to the process of becoming so restrictive and uptight about performance that the person actually diminishes his chances of success. An executive who repeatedly suffers from choking is an executive in crisis.

C A S E
S T U D Y

THE EXECUTIVE WITH PERFORMANCE ANXIETY

Roger is a banking executive with a quasi-governmental agency that provides short-term loans to banks and savings and loan associations. Most of his friends think of Roger as gregarious and fun-loving. Around the office, everyone is fond of Roger's affinity for harmless practical jokes.

Roger earned his MBA ten years earlier, and ever since has been angling for a director's position at the agency. On paper, Roger looks like the perfect candidate for a director's position. Recently, several positions came open and Roger eagerly interviewed for each of them. Unfortunately, he was eventually turned down for all of them.

Each of the interview teams had similar comments about Roger. He knows the organization well and is competent at his job. He has good credentials and raving references from bosses, peers, and customers. The problem with Roger, they each noted, was that he performed very poorly during his panel interviews. The process of becoming director requires an interview before a panel of three senior executives. During each of these interviews, Roger had little to say. When he did speak, he came across as defensive and even sarcastic. He would slouch in his chair, hands in his pocket, and stare at his feet for the entire interview. His answers were usually no more than two or three short sentences.

What was surprising to the interviewers was that several of them wanted to give Roger high marks, since they knew of his track record. Yet his performance was so dismal they couldn't do it. The interviewers who didn't know Roger before were mostly dismayed at his off-the-cuff remarks and demeaning manner.

Roger suffered from choking. He had everything he needed to become a director, and when the time came for him to perform, he choked. Roger's experience is very similar to that of other executives who suffer from choking. On an everyday basis, they can handle the job well, but when the spotlight is placed squarely on them, they fail miserably. It's not that they can't handle the performance, it's that they sabotage themselves every time their performance is critical.

Roger is an executive who is stuck in an unresolved crisis. The particular crisis isn't clear at this point, but in later chapters we will discuss the identifying characteristics of each crisis. Simply the fact the Roger suffers from choking, however, is evidence of an unresolved crisis.

Lack of Focus

The executive who suffers from a short attention span and never seems to stick with a project or job long enough to be successful is in crisis. The unfocused executive bounces from project to project, always busy but never accomplishing much of value. This executive may appear to bore easily or be afraid of commitment (we'll discuss these further in Chapter Thirteen on the crisis of commitment). He often appears tired and frazzled from working long hours. For all this executive works, however, very little seems to come out of the effort. Then, for unexplained reasons, he begins to slack off and becomes noticeably disinterested in work.

C A S E
S T U D Y

THE BORED EXECUTIVE

Renee has held a succession of jobs in the sales field over the past thirty years. In each new position, Renee goes through the cycle of working hard on numerous projects, but she fails to follow any of them through to finality. Eventually, Renee loses interest in her work and begins letting important details slide until eventually she is fired.

One of the typical jobs Renee held was that of sales director for a women's cosmetic company. Initially excited at the prospect of working with other women, Renee jumped into the job with extraordinary energy. She visited all the department stores in her area that sold the cosmetics and spent time with each salesperson. She listened carefully to their concerns about her product and promised them that she would personally handle whatever it was that they needed. In a very short time, Renee's to-do list had grown extremely long. She would jump from one request to the other, never really giving any one project the attention it deserved. Then she would hold a staff meeting and dump many of the unfinished projects on her employees. Before her staff could adequately deal with what she had given them, she moved them over to a new project. Time and again she did this, frustrating everyone who worked for her and disappointing the salespeople to whom she had promised results that never happened.

After about a year of this whirlwind activity, Renee started to come in late in the mornings and take off Mondays and Fridays. She seemed tired, and rather than being out in the field as she had been, she stayed mostly in her office with the doors closed. When the time came for her second-year performance review, Renee's boss was forced to deny her a pay raise and suggested that she get some help.

Renee's lack of focus and on-again, off-again approach to

her job is characteristic of an executive in crisis. Although she may blame her problems on the job and believe that the next one will be different, close examination shows that she is stuck in a repeating pattern. Until Renee is willing to confront and resolve the crisis, she will likely continue this pattern no matter what job she takes.

The Promise Breaker

The executive who is a promise breaker will make commitments, sign contracts, and then, if it suits his purpose, break them without much warning. His word is essentially meaningless as his commitment always shifts to the highest bidder.

Of course, promise breaking will ultimately be disastrous to an executive's career, but in the short term, if he keeps moving from job to job, he can survive. The most damaging aspect of the promise breaker's behavior is that his peers lose respect and trust for him. The promise-breaking executive is generally unaware that he has lost the support of others, and he may even be perplexed at why others have distanced themselves from him.

C A S E
S T U D Y

BROKEN PROMISES, BROKEN TRUST

Matt was the manager of public relations for a large high-tech company. Part of his job included the production of the company's in-house magazine and a monthly video report from the CEO that was distributed throughout the company and to select stock market analysts. Matt saw himself as a public relations expert and was somewhat embarrassed by his employment with a corporation. In his mind, he should have been a high-flying executive at an advertising firm or public relations house. Better yet, he imagined himself best suited as an independent public relations consultant working with high-profile personalities and politicians.

In the two years that Matt had held his position, he had broken the contract for the company's magazine three times. Each time, he would find some superfluous reason to dump the current agreement and switch to another contractor.

Matt was always courting public relations firms that were seeking contract business with his company. His ulterior motive was that he was trying to make connections outside the company so that he might be able to obtain a true public relations job. He would meet with almost any contractor or consultant who called upon him, and if he thought they might be able to help him, he'd find a way to give them some business. Consequently, he moved the company's magazine from contractor to contractor, looking for one that might offer him a job.

Matt didn't realize that his reputation in the public relations field was greatly affected by his behavior. Everyone knew he was unreliable and a promise breaker, and while they might try to court him for whatever business he would throw their way, they would never even consider hiring him.

Promise breakers often think they are constantly "trading up," but more often than not they are only hurting their reputations and chances for advancement. One of the most essential ingredients to advancement is trust, and when that is broken, an executive, no matter how talented, has little to offer.

The Loner

The loner executive tries to accomplish his job completely independent of others. While this characteristic is often associated with the crisis of isolation, it can also be a component of other crises. The loner executive has stopped trying to network within his company or his field, and often expresses a subtle mistrust and cynicism about working with others. He expects employees to cheat, be lazy, or be unreliable. He thinks his peers are only concerned about their own welfare and will do whatever is necessary to further their own careers.

Here's how one employer described the experience of employing a loner executive:

> John is a twenty-five veteran of our industry. He is an affable, well-educated, and responsible person with a quick mind and excellent sales skills. I guess it was ten years ago that I first met him at a national trade show. He mentioned to me then that he was interested in changing jobs, so we kept in touch for the next few years.
>
> Two years later, John showed up in my office one afternoon. He was noticeably agitated and told me how he was getting "screwed" by his current employer. The way he described it, the place sounded miserable and I sympathized with his need to get out. So I basically created a position for him at our company, figuring that we could use another pair of hands, and that eventually he would create enough business to justify his salary.
>
> John did a great job in the field selling consulting projects. Several clients called to tell me how much they enjoyed working with John and what a great job he was doing. I passed these comments along to John and congratulated him on having such great client relations. I also mentioned to him that I noticed he wasn't paying as much attention to planning the work he was selling. After all, I reminded him, we had to make sure we could actually handle the business he was selling.
>
> Over the next year, John's lack of planning seemed to get worse, not better. He would sell services that we just didn't have the manpower to fulfill and force us to subcontract the work, greatly diminishing our profit margin. Whenever we discussed the problem, he'd complain that we weren't backing him up, and it wasn't his problem. I tried every way I knew to help him see the predicament his Lone Ranger–style

of working was causing, but it just didn't sink in. He'd end up getting mad and walking out.

Once one of our senior partners got a call about a project that John was working on and called John to get some information on it. Apparently, John ranted and raved about how he wasn't getting any support and really tore into the senior partner.

After that incident, John became increasingly difficult to work with. He absolutely refused to work by company guidelines if they didn't suit his purpose. Finally, we had no choice but to let him go. Afterward, we learned that John had been let go by no fewer than four previous employers for similar behavior. Three years after we fired him, I learned at a conference that John had been let go by yet another firm.

The case of John illustrates well the plight of the loner executive. He may produce results, but his unwillingness to cooperate makes his life extremely difficult. Like John, he is full of blame toward everyone who doesn't support him, isn't competent, and so on. He sees himself as always getting a raw deal.

The loner executive is an executive in crisis. His isolation and blame are defense mechanisms he uses to avoid dealing with his own crisis, and he shifts the anxiety he feels about himself onto others.

Irresistible Impulse

The executive who engages in the irresistible impulse is in crisis. For unexplained reasons, he does something that is blatantly inappropriate. Years ago, when I was a managing a corporate organizational development staff, I had a boss who engaged in the irresistible impulse. Although he knew very well that sexual references in conversations with employees was strictly off-limits (he had even led programs on sexual harassment), he couldn't help but do so whenever he was with employees in a casual setting. One time, he went a step too far:

One evening after the entire department had been at an offsite meeting, several of the development staff met the boss for dinner at a restaurant that overlooked the Pacific on a particularly beautiful stretch of California coast. He started up conversation with one of my staff members. I didn't hear the first part of the conversation, but my ears perked up when I heard him refer to another woman as "gifted." I knew he wasn't referring to her intellect, and it was apparent that my female employee knew it, too. She looked horrified that he would say such a thing and replied sarcastically, "I don't get it . . . was she really smart?" My boss then proceeded to describe in detail what he was referring to: the woman's large breasts.

I couldn't believe my ears. I tried to intervene in the conversation, but there was no stopping him. He kept on with the sexual banter until finally my employee walked out in disgust. Two weeks later, he was rightfully served with a sexual harassment complaint.

Why did my boss do it? Of course he knew better. It was the irresistible impulse that kept him going—the unconscious desire to sabotage his own success. Like my boss, executives who engage in the irresistible impulse are trying to suppress a crisis, and the irresistible impulse becomes a vent for all the pent-up angst inside them. The thrill of spending petty cash on lottery tickets, cheating on the expense account, or stealing company property is nothing more than a defense mechanism that helps some executives avoid the crisis that is really troubling them.

Extreme Denial

The executive who refuses to acknowledge a serious problem—one that everyone around him sees—is engaged in extreme denial. He may persist in saying that it isn't as bad as everyone else says it is, or worse, simply ignore the problem.

Why would any executive engage in such dangerous behavior? Because acknowledging the problem situation and dealing with it may also require him to deal with a crisis that he is actively and persistently suppressing. Dealing with the problem is just too threatening to him personally, so he chooses to ignore it, and hopes that the situation will somehow take care of itself.

C A S E
S T U D Y

CONFUSING CHANGE WITH A PERSONAL THREAT

Don is the executive director of an organization that provides hospice care for patients infected with the HIV virus in a large metropolitan city. He's led the organization for fifteen years, since the very beginning of the disease, when his organization was seeing hundreds of patients die from AIDS every year. He worked hard in those early days to raise money for the hospice at a time when AIDS was quite misunderstood and considered something of a stigma. He piloted the organization through many tumultuous times.

In the last five years, however, the face of HIV treatment changed dramatically. Drugs that were only recently introduced have diminished deaths from AIDS significantly, and the nature of HIV has shifted from a terminal disease to more of an acute illness.

Don, however, refused to acknowledge the changing trends and continued to try to maintain the organization at the level it was when far more people were dying from the disease. His fund-raising campaigns became more aggressive, and the appeals continued to describe a very dire situation for HIV patients that, in truth, was no longer the case. Instead of addressing the real problem, Don hired the services of a team-building consultant and began a six-month program of building stronger teams in the organization. The program cost a great deal and took large blocks of the staff's time.

Other community leaders working with HIV became concerned that Don's organization was soliciting funds for a service that was no longer in demand. Since the total funds available for HIV in a given community tend to be limited, they felt that more funding should be channeled into purchasing lifesaving but extremely expensive drugs for patients who couldn't afford them. Pressure began to mount on Don, but he continued as if nothing had changed. Eventually, the county and city governments that partially funded Don's organization severely cut back their support. Despite all this, Don continued to maintain the same staffing and overhead expense structure of the organization. Now, Don's organization is deeply in debt and on the verge of closing its doors.

Like so many executives engaged in extreme denial, Don refused to see the obvious changes in his business environment. He tried to convince himself things hadn't really changed all that much, and this was just one more battle he needed to win. The business landscape had changed dramatically with the advent of new drugs, but Don refused to acknowledge that his organization needed to change the services it provided if it was to stay in business.

Don took action in way that was less threatening to him than dealing with the real problem. By taking action, even if it was misguided, Don was able to temporarily relieve his anxiety and feel that progress was being made. Other kinds of actions that executives often make while in denial is to create and fill a new position or launch a large-scale project that consumes their time and attention and does nothing to solve the problem situation.

The new environment meant that Don would have to forge into uncharted territory such as case management or clinical services, but the idea of letting go of the old objectives and moving forward into new areas was personally threatening to

Don. Inwardly, he didn't believe he had the skills to do any-thing else (crisis of self-confidence), so he stuck his head in the sand and hoped that he wouldn't have to change.

Moodiness

Unexplained and persistent moodiness is a sure sign of an exec-utive in crisis. One employee described the moodiness of his boss this way:

> I can't remember exactly when it started, but we all started to notice it last fall. Amy would come into the office in a good mood—I mean, a really good mood. She'd laugh and joke and congratulate us all on a job well done. Then, by afternoon or the next day, she'd be furious over something. We were never sure what would set her off. Without any notice, she'd declare that nothing we did was right, and she'd be stomp-ing around the office, going from one desk to the next telling us how to do our jobs. I know this sounds crazy, but in a few hours she'd be her old self again, pleasant and friendly.

> You can't imagine the havoc her moods caused in the office. When she praised you, you never quite believed it because you knew that it was just a mat-ter of time before she was on your case again. Sometimes when she was in a good mood, she'd make decisions that she would later reverse. We got to where we just tried to avoid her and keep our heads low. Some of the staff complained to her boss, but it just sounded like we were whining. Finally, I couldn't take the craziness anymore and transferred out of her department. In no time, most of the staff either did the same or quit.

Frequent and noticeable shifts in mood are usually expressions of anxiety that is troubling an executive. Fits of anger followed by compensating periods of ingratiating pleasantness is a cycle that some executives who are suffering from an inflamed crisis find themselves repeating. The result is that the executive begins to appear unpredictable and others begin to lose trust in his ability to lead.

Indecisiveness

Another clear expression of the anxiety of an executive in crisis is persistent indecisiveness. Overwhelming anxiety can block the executive's otherwise rational decision processes and cause him to avoid making needed decisions. In severe cases, the executive becomes so incapacitated that even the most basic, everyday decisions become excruciatingly difficult.

C A S E
S T U D Y

AN UNIDENTIFIED CRISIS WILL REMAIN UNRESOLVED

Daniel was a purchasing director for a midsize manufacturing company. Shortly after being passed over for a promotion, Daniel began allowing purchase orders to stack up on his desk. Usually, Daniel would approve or deny a purchase order the same day it was submitted. Now he was laboring over each one and taking days and sometimes weeks before he would respond. Department heads throughout the company became increasingly frustrated with the delays, and soon even assembly-line operations were delayed because needed materials couldn't be purchased without Daniel's approval.

Daniel's descent into indecisiveness was a symptom of something more troubling in his life. While on the surface it appeared that he needed help organizing his work and with decision making, the real issue was his unresolved crisis, a far more personal and complex problem that would benefit greatly from coaching.

PART
TWO

Transactional Coaching

This next session is a brief visit to the more abstract world of psychological theory. While the material may seem a bit unusual for a business book, it is absolutely crucial to understanding the process of executive coaching. Take your time and read through Chapters Five through Eight carefully. Understanding and then translating these loftier psychological concepts into the more pragmatic world of business is the gift of the truly successful executive coach.

FIVE

UNDERSTANDING THE EXECUTIVE EGO

There are many models of coaching, but the most effective with executives in crisis comes from a theory called *transactional analysis*, or just *TA*. TA was popularized in the late 1960s and early 1970s through the publication of a couple of best-selling books, namely, *Games People Play* by Eric Berne and *I'm OK—You're OK* by Thomas Harris. Both Berne and Harris were highly trained psychiatrists in the field of psychoanalysis who became frustrated with the lack of results psychoanalysis often achieved in patients. After years of treatment that often included four one-hour sessions each week, patients saw little progress. Berne and Harris began investigating other methods that could capitalize on the benefits of psychoanalysis, but also be of maximum help to their patients.

The result of their work, TA, was an easily understood and quickly applied model that seemed to help patients through the crises in their lives. In the years that followed the first publications about TA, academic and medical research began to confirm the positive results of TA with nonpsychotic populations.

In recent years, TA has often been criticized for its vernacular approach to difficult subjects. For example, in "OK" TA refers to the existential condition of man, and "games" refers to complex and defensive behaviors. Because of its popularity and influence on the pop lingo of the 1970s, TA is inextricably linked with that decade. Nevertheless, most criticism of TA has come from those wishing to hide psychological truths behind a mystical veil that can only be interpreted by those educated in the profession. In terms of practical results, all research indicates that TA is highly effective in creating positive behavioral change.

I have chosen to use TA as an executive coaching model for two important reasons. First, because unlike most psychological theories, it isn't "disease based." TA assumes that human beings are basically "OK" and capable of making substantial behavioral change if they have the right tools. Most other models assume that problematic behavior is rooted in psychological disability or illness and, as a result, is very difficult to change. Second, for most people, TA uses a language that is accessible and based in common sense. Rather than postulating on hypothetical constructs such as the id or superego, TA talks about the internalized child or parent. You will find that most executives more easily accept the concepts of TA and apply them to their lives for positive change.

The basic assumption of TA is that a person has three ego states: parent, adult, and child. These ego states are identifiable states of being that are produced by the playback of events recorded in memory. For example, the parent ego state is the sum total of a person's memory of his parents from birth until about age five or six. This memory is unedited and unquestioned. The child ego state, in contrast, is based on the unedited and unquestioned memory of the child's internal feelings and thoughts from that same period. Finally, the adult ego state begins to develop in late childhood and continues throughout life. It is the rational decision-making ego state that perceives reality and processes it, much like a computer might objectively process data.

Using these three ego states, you can understand the crises of your client and help him find resolution to those crises. While TA is often used to understand communication between two people, such as a manager and employee, it is also helpful and perhaps more insightful as a tool to understand the dynamics in the mind of a single executive. Since each ego state can operate autonomously, the internal dialogue between ego states determines much of an executive's behavior—particularly during a crisis. To understand how this happens, let's look at each ego state more carefully.

The Parent

The parent ego state is a repository of experiences or "tapes" of his parents or parent surrogates. Everything the child saw his parents do and everything he heard them say is recorded in the Parent. The Parent is highly specific to each person, resulting from his unique childhood experience. What my parent contains and what your parent contains differ to the extent that different parents raised us and consequently we have different memories.

The parent ego state can be summarized as the internal, unexamined "how to" guide. Why do you always make up your bed in the morning? Why do you always look for the lowest price on gasoline? These may be unexamined how-to rules that are directly inherited from your parent. The Parent is the internal instructional guide that is the home of "should" and "ought" as well as the tendency to nurture or "parent" others.

Examples of your parent in action include statements such as:

"You should go to church on Sunday."

"You must be gainfully employed, even if you don't need the salary."

"You must not be a failure."

"You aren't very smart."

"Let me help you with that."

Within the Parent are two very special kinds of instruction sets. They are *attributions* and *injunctions*. Attributions are statements made by the real parent that ascribe certain qualities to the child. For example: "You're the good son," or "You'll never be as talented as your sister," or "You're going to be a big success."

Attributions are extremely powerful influences on a child that continue to shape the child's life into adulthood. Particularly powerful are attributions that are made to a third party in the presence of the child. The famed British psychiatrist and master therapist R. D. Laing writes eloquently on the subject of this kind of attribution:

> One way to get someone to do what one wants, is to give an order. To get someone to be what one wants him to be, or supposes he is or is afraid he is (whether or not this is what one wants), that is, to get him to embody one's projection, is another matter. In a hypnotic (or similar) context, one does not tell him what to be, but tells him what he is. Such attributions, in context, are many times more powerful than orders (or other forms of coercion or persuasion). An instruction need not be defined as an instruction. It is my impression that we receive most of our earliest and most lasting instructions in the form of attributions. We are told such and such is the case. One is, say, told one is a good or a bad boy or girl, not only instructed to be a good or bad boy or girl. One may be subject to both, but if one is (this or that), it is not necessary to be told to be what one has already been "given to understand" one is. The key medium for communication of this kind is probably not verbal language. When attributions have the function of instructions or injunctions, this function may be denied, giving rise to one type of mysti-

fication, akin to, or identical with, hypnotic suggestion . . . .

One may tell someone to feel something and not to
remember he has been told. Simply tell him he feels
it. Better still, tell a third party, in front of him, that
he feels it.[1]

The executive's internal Parent is alive with attributions
from his childhood. Some of these may have a very positive effect
on his behavior and ultimate success; others—and these are
often the subject of coaching—can be extremely detrimental.

The other form of instruction contained in the Parent are
injunctions. If attributions are telling a child who he is, then
injunctions are telling a child who he is not or what not to do.
Examples might include:

"Don't show your feelings."

"Never fail."

"Never give up."

"Don't enjoy life."

Injunctions may or may not be verbal. The example of the
parents very often establishes an injunction without it ever being
spoken. Such injunctions as "Never forgive someone for hurting
you" or "Never apologize for committing a wrong" are likely to
have never been spoken by the parent but acted out.
Consequently, nonverbal injunctions are just as powerful. The
child, watching the parent's example, learns and internalizes the
injunction.

Finally, the Parent also contains the nurturing instincts
inherited from the real parent's behavior. The urge to protect,
help, and even rescue come from this part of the internal Parent.
An executive acting out of this part of his Parent may say things
like: "Let me help you with that project," or "You're not quite
ready to handle that customer yet," or "If you have any questions, just come and ask me, and I can answer them for you."

A person responds to his internal Parent in one of three
ways:

1. He unconsciously follows the Parent's instructions.

2. He unconsciously rebels against the Parent's instructions.

3. He consciously examines the Parent's instructions and then chooses whether he will allow it to influence his behavior.

The first two responses are automatic. The executive either follows the internal dictates of his Parent (as a good child) or he rebels against it (as a rebellious and difficult child) and does the opposite. Either way, he is not choosing his behavior, but reacting to the internal Parent. Even when he is rebelling against the Parent, the Parent is still controlling his behavior.

Many clients who seek therapy, read self-help books, attend leadership seminars, or receive coaching find themselves tempted to rebel against the Parent. In other words, if the Parent is morally rigid and narrow, the client deliberately becomes amoral. Or, if the Parent is demanding that he succeed, then he deliberately fails. The client who rebels is not truly choosing his behavior, but reacting to the dictates of his internal Parent.

The third response is the reaction of the executive who leads an examined life. Either from coaching, therapy, or life experience he has learned that certain instincts and behavior reflexes come from material he internalized many years ago from his parents. He does not have to follow those urges if he chooses not to. The critical point here is that he must become *aware* of the influence of his Parent before he has a choice to follow it or not.

The Child

The child ego state is usually the most repressed of all the ego states in an executive. Since much of the Child is formed before language skills are mastered, it contains primarily feelings. These feelings are associated with specific memories and, later in life, can be triggered by similar experiences. For example, the executive may feel overwhelmingly ashamed when questioned by a superior. Such feelings are the feelings of a child being shamed for naughty behavior.

What's important to remember is that the Child is recorded "straight," without editing. In other words, the experience of the child is recorded without modification or explanation. Why? Because a child isn't capable of such mental gymnastics yet. For example, a child isn't capable of understanding why his parents are arguing. He simply records the memory of the terror he felt when they argued. The fear experienced by watching the two persons on whom he is dependent for survival attack one another is recorded directly into his memory banks without any explanation, such as when his father is angry because he just discovered that his business deal has gone down the drain.

Not only does the Child contain feelings of fear, it also contains wonderful feelings of discovery and revelation. As the young child experiences the world for the first time, he is fascinated and gratified by many things that older humans take for granted. These feelings of creativity and discovery are firmly rooted in the Child.

The fact that memories are recorded directly and uncensored into the Child is significant because it is the job of the healthy Adult to examine the contents of the Child and decide what is realistic and appropriate. For the executive in crisis, examining the triggered feelings from the Child is key to crisis resolution.

Like he does with the Parent, the executive can follow, rebel against, or examine the dictates of his internal Child. If his Child is playful and impulsive, he may either become playful and impulsive or rebel and become stern and matter-of-fact. On the other hand, if this executive has learned to examine the contents of his Child, he may choose to be playful if it is appropriate, or ignore the impulse if the situation demands otherwise. Conscious examination of the internal Child and Parent is an important step on the road to resolving life's crises.

The Adult

The Adult is the rational part of the personality. The Adult perceives information in the present and then processes that information in order to direct behavior. The Adult begins to emerge in the personality during the later years of childhood and continues to emerge throughout life.

The Adult is primarily concerned with processing emotional information in an objective, almost scientific fashion. It is different from the Parent, which is "judgmental in an imitative way and seeks to enforce sets of borrowed standards, and from the Child, which tends to react more abruptly on the basis of pre-logical thinking and poorly differentiated or distorted perceptions."[2]

The Adult can be thought of as a computer that arrives at a decision after mechanically combining emotional information. The Adult processes emotional (as opposed to intellectual) data from the three ego states: the Parent, the Child, and the data that the Adult has gathered. As noted earlier, one of the important functions of the Adult is to examine information in the Parent in order to see whether that information is true and still appropriate for today. Likewise, the Adult examines the information in the Child to see whether the feelings there are appropriate to the present, obsolete, or merely a knee-jerk reaction to unexamined commands issued from the Parent. In the poetic words of Ralph Waldo Emerson, the Adult "must not be hindered by the name of goodness, but must examine if it be goodness."

Sometimes it is easy to confuse intellectual functioning with that of the Adult. To understand the difference, think of a child prodigy such as Wolfgang Amadeus Mozart as depicted in the theatrical play and movie *Amadeus*. Mozart as a child was a musical genius of spectacular proportions who was also given to having tantrums, playing practical jokes, and childishly romping about at inappropriate times. Mozart's musical intellect was extraordinary, but even as he entered adulthood, he was almost solely driven by his internal Child ego state. In similar fashion, it is quite possible for a brilliant executive to regularly have tantrums, rant, and childishly insult employees. His intellect is excellent, but his internal Child controls his emotions.

The Adult also contains an emotional component called *passion*. Passion is much more than merely joy or attraction, as felt by the Child. It is a complex emotion that is enduring and grows the more a person experiences it. Passion is the source of persistence and strength toward a goal when attainment is long and difficult. It short, it is enduring inspiration.

The discovery of passion and following where it leads is the ultimate fulfillment of the Adult. When the Child and Parent are primarily in control, the Adult is so encumbered as to completely block the discovery of passion. Only once the Adult has examined the content and control of both the Parent and the Child can it begin to birth passion within the individual.

The passion component of the Adult is extremely important to becoming a high-achieving executive. Again and again we will return to function of the Adult in the experience of passion within the executive. Full emotional engagement is fulfilled only once passion is discovered and allowed to lead.

The difference between the functions of the three ego states can best be summarized thusly: Through the Adult, a person can begin to tell the difference between life as it was taught and demonstrated to him (Parent), life as he felt it or wished it to be (Child), and life as he figures it out for himself (Adult). The goal of coaching isn't to eliminate the Child or the Parent, but to examine their contents so that they are no longer blindly dictating the executive's behavior. To teach the executive to block either of these ego states would cause great harm to the executive and to his career. The fully functioning person needs all three states to live life to its fullest and achieve all that is possible.

Executive Ego and Crisis

The executive can at any moment be controlled by one and only one of the ego states. Consider this fictitious discussion with a subordinate:

Executive *(Parent)*:
Why do I always have to remind you of deadlines?

Employee *(Child)*:
Because that's your job.

Executive *(Adult)*:
The project is due on March 1.

Employee *(Adult)*:
I'll do my best to have it done by then.

Executive *(Child)*:
It's such a nice day, let's finish our staff meeting outside on the lawn.

In this exchange, the executive has been controlled successively by all three ego states. The changes that might be observed in his behavior, language, and body posture are all clues to the ego state that is in control.

Oftentimes, however, what is more important in coaching the executive in crisis isn't the outward behavior of the ego states, but the inner dialogue between the ego states. For example, the executive with a strong Parent that continually belittles him for not achieving more will likely experience the feelings that are evoked from his Child of shame and lowered self-confidence.

One of the important insights into coaching is that *behavior is often determined by the dynamic between ego states.* In other words, the executive may be acting out the Child as a result of the interaction between his internal Parent and Child. It is in the internal dynamic between ego states that the richest coaching material emerges. This is where both the beginning of crisis and the resolution of crisis exist. In later chapters we will look at the internal dynamic between ego states that likely creates each crisis.

Stimulation, Recognition, and Structure

The bottom line of life is that we are all seeking stimulation, recognition, and structure. Stimulation is sensory excitement, including most importantly human touch. The landmark study by René Spitz in the 1940s established that children raised in hospitals and orphanages where they were deprived of human touch eventually experienced deterioration of their central nervous system, a condition that can eventually lead to death.

What is commonly called boredom is the condition of stimulus deprivation. We call ourselves bored whenever we have habituated (i.e., become insensitive through familiarity) to the ordinary stimulation in our environment or are generally deprived of stimulation. To avoid boredom, we will sometimes behave in strange ways or even against our own self-interest just to generate the stimulation we crave. Executives have been known to destroy their careers to alleviate boredom. Later, as we begin to explore the games that executives play, the value of stimulation, even when it is detrimental to the executive's career, becomes an important factor.

Like stimulation, recognition can be positive (i.e., a compliment) or negative (i.e., a reprimand). Obviously, we prefer positive recognition but will accept negative recognition when nothing else is available. We have a burning existential need for acknowledgment, and we seek it daily.

There are many ways we may seek recognition: through hard work, friendly behavior, relationships, and overt attention-seeking actions, to name just a few. One special way in which we seek recognition is through what TA calls *games*. Games are a special kind of activity that on the surface appear to do one thing, but underneath have the specific purpose of winning either positive or negative recognition.

Finally, structure is the need for some predictability. We need routines and rituals that are familiar. Even when we are seeking new stimulation, we want to do it through established rituals such as going to a cocktail party, a movie, or museum. We want to find the unexpected in expected ways.

Executives can often been seen desperately seeking structure, particularly in industries such as high technology that are fast-paced and changing. Executives have become masters at mapping out ideas and conceptual processes on flipcharts for the primary purpose of discovering familiar structure. For example, labeling a sales slowdown the result of an "overheated economy" or a product failure as "market saturation" seems to impose structure on both of these unexpected events. By using familiar terms to label situations, we convince ourselves that what we are seeing is familiar and predictable.

Games

Eric Berne, who wrote the classic book *Games People Play*, has defined a game as "a recurring set of transactions, often repetitive, superficially rational, with a concealed motivation; or, more colloquially, as a series of transactions with a gimmick."[3] To summarize, there are three basic conditions that define a game:

1. An ongoing series of transactions that have an ostensible social reason

2. An ulterior motive for earning recognition

3. A predictable payoff that concludes the game and is the
real purpose for playing

Berne has identified many games, many of which are discussed in detail in Chapter Eight. Here are a few examples:

❖ *Kick Me.* This is a game where the executive deliberately
does or says something wrong in order to earn negative
recognition. On the surface, it seems punishing, but in
reality it is fulfilling the executive's need for recognition.

❖ *Why Don't You, Yes But . . .* This is a game that was stud-
ied in depth by Berne and is common in traditional helping relationships between, say, a minister and congregant
or a counselor and client. The game is played by the
executive when he asks for help then negates every helpful suggestion with a "yes, but . . ." comment. In this
game, the payoff for the executive is to prove that he is
helpless (and to elicit positive recognition in the form of
sympathy from the helper), not to actually receive help.
For example:

Executive:

I can't seem to win the support of senior management.

Coach:

Have you tried calling a meeting to present your ideas?

Executive:

Yes, but no one was available for a month.

Coach:

What about doing something by e-mail or online?

Executive:

That might work except several of the SVPs don't check
their e-mail often.

Coach:

Have you discussed this with your boss and asked for
his help?

Executive:
I mentioned it to him, but he just didn't seem to have the time to help me.

❖ *Now I've Got You, You SOB.* This game is played by the executive to prove his superiority over another person, most often an employee. The game is played when the executive sets up an impossible situation and then waits for the employee to fail. When this happens, the executive comes down hard on the employee, proclaiming something like, "You can never do anything right and probably should be fired!" In this game, the executive sets up the failure situation in order to vent excessive rage at the employee and prove that he (the executive) is superior.

Later in this book, Chapter Eight discusses in detail the games that executives play. Often, helping an executive to understand the games he is playing is a huge step toward resolving his crisis.

Scripts

Now we arrive at one of the most important concepts in coaching an executive: scripts. A script is a plan for one's life that is usually adopted at very young age. For the most part, the script is preconscious, and while it may be familiar to the person, it is often not recognized to be the guiding force of his life. Scripts are very powerful, and their effects can often been seen when you examine the careers of executives in crisis.

The origin of a script usually comes from the internal Parent. In this scenario, a repeated injunction or attribution is adopted as the basis for the script that governs the child's life through adulthood. Until the script and its roots in the Parent are examined, the script can continue to control a person's entire life.

The core idea behind a particular script is often very simple. For example:

"No matter how good it gets, I will eventually screw it up."

"Most everyone is more talented than I am."

"I am destined for greatness."

"People like me."

"I don't get along with most people."

"I can solve most any problem."

These ideas probably entered the child's awareness as an injunction or attribution from the real parents and, consequently, were stored in the Parent. Depending on the force, frequency, and rewards associated with the injunction or attribution, it may have gathered enough psychological power to become a guiding force throughout life.

Why does an executive coach care about scripts? For the simple reason that a crisis is often the "climax" of the script. In other words, the crisis has been building throughout the executive's entire life as a latent crisis and finally culminates as an inflamed crisis.

Have you ever wondered why certain storylines—such as from Shakespeare or *Grimm's Fairy Tales*—burrow themselves deep into the human psyche? These primal stories mimic the scripts that many people live and as such are very familiar to us on an unconscious level. The plot makes sense to us because we've seen it acted out in real life many times before. The truth is, the really great writers are often the great thinkers on the subject of human behavior. The craft of writing a great tale is often one of translating a life script from reality into descriptive language.

I was recently struck by the power of life scripts while reading the life story of the famed French actress Sarah Bernhardt. Bernhardt was arguably the first international celebrity from the entertainment field. Throughout her career she played over seventy roles in more than 125 productions, including over twenty traditional male roles (Hamlet, for instance). She was wined and dined by the world's greatest nobility and wealthiest patrons including Sigmund Freud, who kept a picture of her in his waiting room; Mark Twain, who hailed her as one of the great actresses of all time; and the railroad magnate William Vanderbilt, who attended every one of her New York performances of *Camille*, weeping openly into a large handkerchief. Her picture regularly appeared in newspapers and publications around the globe.

Such fame was quite a feat for a woman who was born in 1844 to a Dutch-Jewish woman who was a highly paid courtesan and who never knew who Sarah's father was. Bernhardt was an emotionally unstable, sickly child who seemed to run a constant temperature and frequently spat up blood. Doctors diagnosed her with a wasting disease (like tuberculosis). At age fifteen, she heard them tell her mother that she would probably have only a few years to live and would never leave the house again.

That attribution so affected Bernhardt that she vehemently rebelled against it for the rest of her life. In her memoir *My Double Life*, she tells how she adopted the lifelong motto *Quand même*, meaning "in spite of everything." She was determined to prove her mother and her doctors wrong at all costs. She did. Sarah Bernhardt died in 1923 at the age of seventy-eight.

Sarah Bernhardt's life was tumultuous and relentlessly driven. At a very young age she had adopted a life script that was an open rebellion against a morbid attribution from her mother and doctors.

A script can control and determine the outcome of an executive's career. Until the script is examined and its roots deep in the Parent of the executive exposed, it has tremendous power to determine the destiny of an executive. Probably the most life-changing work a coach can embark on is the exposure and emancipation of an executive from a detrimental script.

There are three major components to every life script: a *fear complex, games*, and *crises*. Crises are the painfully dramatic periods where the script reaches a climax. So far, we've talked about crises generally and in Part Three of this book will explore them in great depth. Games and fear complexes we'll explore fully in separate chapters.

Emancipating the Executive

The ultimate goal of coaching an executive is to free him from the restraining and detrimental influences of his unexamined Parent and Child that determine his life script. By engaging his Adult and encouraging him to examine the determining contents of his Parent and Child, you restore him to free choice. The emancipated executive *chooses* his career and is no longer driven solely by the unconscious forces of his script. He follows the dictates of his reason, passion, and values. Those alone determine his behavior. This is the executive who reliably makes the best business decisions and, on a daily basis, is inspired and energetic.

Emancipation is the difference between a script-driven and passion-inspired executive. The driven executive is often stressed out and feels as if work is a constant battle with the boss, employees, customers, organizational regulations, government, and so on. The emancipated executive makes choices—some good and others bad—but it is these choices and their consequences that guide his behavior instead of the outdated information stored in the Parent and reacted to by the Child.

Notes

1. Ronald D. Laing, *The Politics of the Family and Other Essays* (New York: Pantheon Books, 1971), p. 105.
2. Eric Berne, *Games People Play* (New York: Ballantine Books, reprinted 1996), p. 96.
3. Eric Berne, "Transactional Analysis," *Active Psychotherapy*, Harold Greenwald, ed. (New York: Atherton Press, 1967), p. 125.

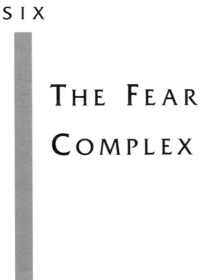

S I X

THE FEAR
COMPLEX

If emancipation from limiting scripts and games is the key to a fully functioning, successful executive, why does he allow himself to stay trapped? What is the block that keeps him from being inspired, committed, and passionate about his work?

At the core of each crisis is a fear that has gradually

become all-consuming. In a previous book, *The Fearless Executive*,[1] I look closely at some of these fears and how they affect the executive's life and career. The emerging research on coaching executives shows that fear plays a significant undermining role in the derailment of otherwise promising and successful executive careers.

The Fear Complex

The underlying dynamic that keeps an executive locked into a damaging script is fear. Fear is an emotion that most often springs from the Child and is the result of the dynamic between the punishing Parent and the vulnerable Child. This is always the source of fear when it isn't coming from the Adult assessing real danger in the present tense, such as fear of imminent bodily harm.

The fear that drives a script and its associated crisis is a fear that has become self-sustaining and continues to consume greater amounts of the executive's energy; it is what I call a *fear complex*. A fear complex is a fear that is no longer connected with any immediate danger and has embedded itself in the consciousness of the executive. In fact, the original fear may have resulted from an event that happened many years ago and the danger is long since past. Even though there is no real danger, the fear continues to grow and color the executive's awareness.

For example, the crisis of individuation is driven by a fear complex of abandonment that comes from the Child fearing abandonment from the protection of the Parent. As a grownup, there is no real danger of being abandoned, yet the fear persists. Every interaction and relationship becomes an opportunity to silence this fear of abandonment by engaging the attention and approval of other persons. When there are disagreements or even signs of possible rejection, it is overinterpreted as impending abandonment, and this causes great anxiety. To silence the anxiety and maintain some sense of equilibrium, a person focuses his attention on winning back approval, smoothing ruffled feathers, and keeping himself in the good graces of all around him.

A fear complex has several distinctive characteristics. First, it is a closed loop, a self-sustaining fear. This means that once a fear complex develops, it perpetuates itself until there is direct intervention to stop it.

A fear complex causes the executive to "cook the books" of his own perception in a way that validates and feeds the fear. For example, a fear complex of abandonment causes the executive to feel great relief whenever he has resolved a conflict with another and won his approval. This is how it works:

1. The executive senses potential abandonment through conflict or disapproval from another person.

2. The fear causes the executive to experience a great deal of anxiety.

3. The executive acts to relieve the anxiety by appeasing the other person and resolving the conflict.

4. The executive is rewarded by a feeling of relief.

5. The feeling of relief wrongly confirms the false assumption that real danger has been averted, and thereby reinforces and perpetuates the fear.

The truth is that there was no real danger of abandonment, but the relief from anxiety made the executive feel as if real danger had been avoided. This fear complex becomes self-sustaining because it never allows the executive to experience what is being avoided. In other words, the executive never allows disagreements or conflicts with others to persist, so he never learns that conflict with others doesn't necessarily lead to abandonment. In fact, healthy conflict can actually lead to respect and stronger relationships, but this executive can't break out of his fear complex to experience them. As a result, the fear perpetuates a kind of false learning.

Learning to recognize a fear complex and all the subtle ways in which it can consume an executive's awareness is a critical skill to being a successful executive coach. If you're not vigilant, an executive can convince you that there really is danger that is driving him to do what he is doing. The organization really is cutthroat and out to get him. It really is important to have *everyone's* approval before he moves forward on the project. He really has been shafted by most of the people he's worked with, and there isn't anyone he can depend on. The evidence he may choose to present can be quite compelling.

Don't be misled. When you see that an executive is being pushed by fear, no matter how convincing a case he makes, rather than making informed choices about his behavior, he is under the influence of a fear complex.

Managing Fear (Instead of the Business)

One of the most distinct features of a fear complex is that the executive makes a management style out of managing fear. Much of what he does is directly or indirectly related to avoiding whatever is feared and keeping his anxiety to a manageable level. Managing the fear complex is what moves a crisis from inflamed to suppressed. Rather than suffer the anxiety of the inflamed crisis and its associated fear, the executive chooses to manage the fear and thereby suppress the crisis.

Once you become attuned to the process of managing a fear complex, you'll be surprised at how quickly you will recognize it in your executive clients. The signs are almost always apparent if you know what to look for. Just a few of them include:

- ❖ Spending excessive time on managing the reactions of others

- ❖ Actively sabotaging the projects of colleagues who threaten your sense of security in the organization

- ❖ Not allowing employees to share the spotlight

- ❖ Adopting an overly cynical attitude about corporate or other staff/personnel programs

- ❖ Adopting a rigid, unyielding refusal to change

- ❖ Attempting to dominate meetings and discussions

- ❖ Adopting a we've-tried-that-before-and-it-won't-work attitude toward most new initiatives

- ❖ Working either excessively long hours or noticeably increasing absences

In later chapters, as we look at each crisis individually and its associated fear complex, we'll discuss the signs of each fear complex as it might appear in the executive's day-to-day activities.

Managing a fear complex in an effort to suppress a crisis locks an executive into a defeating behavioral pattern that he keeps repeating regardless of the consequences.

C A S E
S T U D Y

THE SELF-FOCUSED, EMOTIONALLY UNENGAGED EXECUTIVE

Bob was the director of organizational development for an organization of about 20,000 employees. He was exceptionally driven to prove to senior management that he was a competent and promising executive. The projects that Bob chose to undertake were highly visible projects that would win him the attention and approval he wanted. Other needed projects that weren't so prominent or held some potential for failure, Bob avoided.

Two years after being hired into his position from another company, most of Bob's peers had discovered that the only way to get services from Bob or his department was to make sure there was something in it for Bob. Otherwise, their request would go unheeded.

As you can imagine, this created a great deal of resentment among his peers. Organizational development work that was desperately needed, but didn't help to achieve Bob's personal goals of advancement and power, remained undone. A few executives were even forced to hire outside consultants to do work that Bob wasn't interested in undertaking. For example, the customer service department hired a consultant to help reorganize the four telephone centers around the new customer accounts computer system, and the accounting department was forced to hire an outside consultant to redesign its workflow to be more efficient.

It's important to know that Bob always had a good explanation for his choices. He could spin the corporate phrases and lingo together to create any rationale that suited his purpose. Bob was a formidable competitor and loved to engage in a verbal sparring match.

The day came when the senior management team began talking to Bob about a possible reorganization of the manufacturing division (the largest division in the company). Bob jumped at the opportunity to work on such a large-scale project.

Bob hired one of the best-known management consulting firms to work with him on the project. Together, he and the consultants redesigned the manufacturing division under the project title of "Factory of the Future." The plan they came up with was a state-of-the-art, radical program for change compared with the way the company's manufacturing division was currently operating.. For starters, it required a completely new organizational structure and management information system

Within the reorganization plan, Bob included a significant increase to his own department. With an eye toward a more powerful position for himself, Bob proposed doubling his department by taking the entire quality control department and merging it under his management, thereby increasing his responsibility, title, salary, and power in the organization.

The senior management team, shocked at such an aggressive reorganization plan, allowed Bob to test the plan in one of the company's six manufacturing facilities. A bit disappointed that they hadn't given his plan a standing ovation, Bob forged ahead and began the test implementation.

After a year of testing the plan, it was a dismal failure. Of course, Bob had an explanation for every problem: Not enough funding was provided. Senior management didn't give enough support to the project. Other executives were sabotaging the project. Meanwhile, Bob was quietly escaping to a position at another company.

The problem with Bob was that he wasn't emotionally

engaged with his work and was driven by a fear complex instead. Bob was focused on his strong need to prove himself superior and to become more powerful in the company. As result, his focus was on what might win him attention and approval, rather than what was really right for the company at that time.

Had Bob really been engaged with the project, he would have spent a great deal of time in the manufacturing facilities, learning everything he could about that aspect of the company. He would have talked to assembly-line workers, foremen, and manufacturing engineers to get a complete picture of the problem. This kind of research, however, wasn't flashy and didn't promise to win him much of anything in the short term. Instead, Bob opted to hire the big-name consulting firm and propose whiz-bang advances in technology. All of this, he thought, would reflect positively on him.

Emotional Engagement

The case study of Bob illustrates a simple and very important difference between the executive who is emotionally engaged and one who is reacting from a fear complex. The executive who is emotionally engaged cares deeply about the *content* of the work. He cares enough to get his hands dirty and learn everything he can about what he is doing. The executive driven by a fear complex chooses to forgo such things and act upon his personal need instead. For Bob, it was to suggest a reorganization that would capture the attention of powerful senior executives rather than what might work best for the company.

An executive locked in the grip of a crisis isn't free to be emotionally engaged with his work. Instead, he is driven to make decisions that help him manage his personal fear. His focus isn't the content of what he does, but how what he does helps him to manage his anxiety. While the difference between these two approaches at times may seem slight, in the end, the outcomes are radically different.

Some executives complete their entire careers under the influence of a fear complex. They choose to waste great amounts of energy and resources suppressing the crisis and managing fear. There's probably no greater example of such an executive than J. Edgar Hoover.

J. Edgar Hoover dominated the Federal Bureau of Investigation (FBI) from 1924 until his death in 1972 with his trademark suspicion, hypersensitivity, and obsession with control. Much has been written about Hoover since his death, and while there are varying accounts of his life, most experts agree that Hoover was driven by a personal fear of inferiority.

Throughout his reign as chief of the top investigative agency in the country, Hoover continued to waste enormous resources on managing his personal fear—a fear that had nothing to do with threats to national security. For example, Hoover was quick to transfer, suspend, or even fire an agent for even a slight error or off-the-cuff remark. Often he would make such decisions on the spot and without warning. (Such spontaneous firings had the unintended consequence of spreading fear throughout the agency because no one knew who might be fired next.)

When his superior, Attorney General Robert Kennedy, challenged his authority, Hoover struck back at Kennedy, doing everything he could to document and undermine the attorney general's position and authority. Hoover spent enormous resources and man-hours collecting "dirty laundry" on the presidents under whom he served in an effort to protect his position. Later, when President Richard Nixon tried to convince him to retire, Hoover provided Nixon with a sampling of the information he'd collected on previous presidents. Undoubtedly with much to hide, Richard Nixon never again mentioned retirement to the director.

Hoover demanded complete loyalty from his associates, so fearful and doubtful was he of the sincerity of others. Former FBI agent Joseph Schott recalled a time when one of Hoover's assistant directors tried to calm the director after he read an unflattering editorial in *The Washington Post* about the FBI: "I said to the director, Mr. Hoover, if I had known that they were going to print those subversive, communist-inspired lies about you, I would have gone over there and hurled myself bodily into the presses." Hoover later commented triumphantly to friends, "He may not be very smart, but nobody can doubt his loyalty."[2]

Agent Schott goes on to recall: "Under Mr. Hoover, you had to work on the premise that the director was infallible. If you did not really believe this—and of course most employees certainly did not—you nevertheless had to pay lip service to it to survive . . . and, if you were ambitious and desired to rise in the organization, you had to pay a still higher toll in the form of exaggerated sycophantic respect and adulation for him." [3]

Hoover was intolerant of criticism. Whether it was from a newspaper or a man on the street, he was equally threatened by it. Once Hoover overheard a TWA pilot criticize the FBI's handling of a hijacking case. Angry over what he heard, Hoover issued an order forbidding FBI agents to fly on TWA. Likewise, when Hoover thought that the Xerox Corporation wasn't cooperative enough in an investigation, he ordered all Xerox office equipment to be immediately removed from all FBI offices.

While the activities of Hoover make it sound as if he were a paranoid psychotic, it is also important to remember that Hoover was able to maintain a highly popular public image and run one of the largest governmental agencies at the time. The truth is, Hoover was obsessed with managing his fear and did so at great cost to his employer, the taxpayers; that's something no private corporation could have afforded. During the last twenty of his nearly fifty years in office, Hoover was said to have spent most of his time, and the time of his many associates, plotting against the imagined enemies to his office and authority.

While Hoover may have been extreme, the extent to which powerful executives will go to manage their fear can at times be shocking. All under the guise of good corporate citizenship, enormous resources can be wasted on the executive's personal crusades.

The executive coach must become adept at recognizing an executive who is suppressing a crisis and driven by a fear complex. With a little practice, you will begin to recognize the signs quickly in your clients.

Notes

1. Alan Downs, *The Fearless Executive* (New York: AMACOM, 2000).
2. Joseph L. Schott, *No Left Turns: The FBI in Peace and War* (New York: Praeger, 1975), p. 25.
3. Ibid.

SEVEN

COACHING FOR CHANGE

The goal of coaching is to strengthen and enliven the Adult ego state as referee between the Parent and Child ego states. Since a fear complex emerges from the interaction of these two ego states, the Adult is needed to examine content of both, thus breaking the cycle of fear and the life script that is based upon it. The goal isn't to eliminate either the Parent or

Child ego state's influence, but to moderate both and to make the client conscious of the choices he makes.

What does this mean in practical terms of coaching an executive? It means identifying the parental statements that are provoking fear in the executive's Child. Why does this executive feel inferior? Why does he fear abandonment? Why is he overwhelmingly afraid of failure? Each of these fear complexes creates a script and crisis, and they emerge from his Parent and Child. By helping the executive clarify his ego states and to engage the Adult during times of conflict, he can begin to free himself from the crisis.

Ego Maps

To begin the coaching process, it is helpful to create an ego map of your client. There are several forms this map may take, so the following is a description of each map.

THE PARENT DOMINANT EXECUTIVE

The executive whose personality is based mostly on the content of the Parent has an ego map as shown in Figure 7-1.

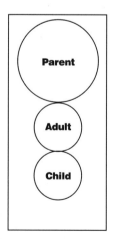

Figure 7-1. The Parent dominant executive.

In this executive, the Parent dominates the personality. He often treats business associates and employees as if they were children. This can manifest through a variety of behaviors the executive has, such as "taking care" of employees, having little sense of humor, being difficult to approach, and focusing on controlling the people around him. In general, this executive works best with two types of people: those willing to be dependent on him, and those willing to subordinate themselves to his control.

The parental executive is most susceptible to the crises of isolation, inferiority, and passion. Among executives who seek coaching, this ego configuration is by far the most common.

The dominant Parent can make the executive feel duty-bound to the organization. He generally adheres to a very clear sense of right and wrong and doesn't tolerate mistakes or ambiguity well. In addition, he may be judgmental, critical of others, moralistic, and somewhat emotionally flat.

Coaching the parental executive centers around enlarging the Adult while minimizing the influence of the Parent. This is done by encouraging the executive to examine his parental responses in a rational way (Adult). For example, the executive who has isolated himself because of intolerance of others' mistakes can be encouraged to examine the rationality of perfection. Since even he isn't perfect, how effective is it for him to hold others to that standard? Further coaching might delve into the origins of his Parent's strict standards. Was he expected to be perfect as child? Has he continued to hold himself to that standard? How does this make him feel about himself? Such questions begin revealing the life script of the executive that has brought him to the crisis of isolation.To continue with this example, it is important that coaching identify the *triggers* of his Parent. Triggers are those events that cause him to automatically respond in a parental mode. What is it that he does or others do that causes him to respond in harsh, moralistic ways? Perhaps it is a small oversight by an employee or a colleague's failure to include him in a budget decision that send him into a parental rage. Whatever the trigger is, coaching helps the executive to identify it so that he can consciously engage his Adult rather than automatically engaging his Parent—in other words, to consciously stop and think about the most rational response to this mistake. How bad is it really? Can it be corrected? Does it even need to be corrected?

Why must he be so enraged by the humanness of himself and other people? Is his parental response helping or hurting the situation?

Then the coach helps the executive identify more Adult ways of handling the situation. Upon examination, the executive realizes that shaming and blaming himself or others is not productive, and consequently, he teaches himself a new, more problem-solving response to mistakes that is free of harsh judgments.

THE CHILD DOMINANT EXECUTIVE

The ego map of the executive whose Child is dominant is shown in Figure 7-2.

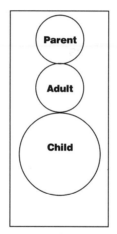

Figure 7-2. The Child dominant executive.

While less common than the Parent dominant executive, the Child dominant executive is seen regularly by executive coaches. In this executive the Child is predominant and causes him to avoid commitment. Instead, he is driven to seek reward and recognition in ways that make him appear impulsive, insecure, vulnerable, and constantly in need of proving himself to his superiors.

This executive acts out of feelings that might be associated with a frightened or joyous child who is subject to tantrums. Of course, when the executive acts these scenarios out, it looks very different than when a child acts them out. The important issue is that the *feeling* driving the behavior is the same.

The Child dominant executive may be easily threatened and intimidated. He reacts by withdrawing or by becoming a bully and attempting to cover up his insecurity with an extra measure of aggression. He may impulsively try to undermine and discredit his critics or make impulsive and risky decisions on the fly. He may also be the executive who becomes inappropriately intoxicated at the company Christmas party and begins harassing his boss's wife or begins an affair with an employee, even though he is well aware of the rules against such liaisons.

This executive may also be well liked and considered one of the "guys." He is the type to fill his office with sports memorabilia and always has a joke to tell. His language is often filled with sports analogies (e.g., "we've got to raise the bar" and "let's hit this one out of the park") or war analogies (e.g., "this is our strategic strike" or "we can't afford a coup d'état in the ranks"). When you talk to this executive, it's not at all difficult to envision a young boy sitting breathlessly at the ballpark or playing war games with his G.I. Joe.

Coaching the Child dominant executive is about strengthening the Adult to moderate the influence of the Child over the executive's behavior. Certain impulses that emerge from the Child are immediately gratifying (e.g., getting drunk at the company Christmas party) but do far more harm in the long-term picture. Imagine handing over your company's most important product line to an executive who can't control himself in a simple social situation. I don't think you or I would do it, and history shows that most companies won't do it, either.

The way to help strengthen the Adult is to first identify the triggers of Child dominant behavior. What is it that happens just before he feels compelled to drink too much at a company affair? Does he feel frightened or socially inadequate? Does he feel a need to gain attention by being the life of the party? These triggers are important to identify because they are warning flags for intervention by the Adult. The next time he feels socially inadequate, he learns through coaching to consciously engage the Adult by asking, "What's the appropriate thing for me to do here?"

Perhaps this process sounds as simple to you as it does to me rereading it on the page. The problem is, it is not simple in practice. The coach must work carefully with the executive to identify the real triggers, not the triggers that he thinks are acceptable. In other words, it may make him feel inadequate to tell the coach that he feels socially inadequate, so instead he finds some other, more socially acceptable trigger. The job of the coach is to relentlessly push until you are both satisfied that you've found the true trigger for his Child dominant behavior.

THE UNDIFFERENTIATED EXECUTIVE

The ego of the undifferentiated executive is shown in Figure 7-3.

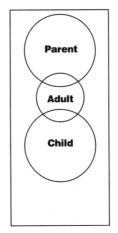

Figure 7-3. The undifferentiated executive.

The undifferentiated executive has an exceptionally weak Adult and makes it through life by bouncing between the parent and child ego states. Obviously this kind of erratic behavior that vacillates between judgmental and emotional outbursts isn't tolerated well in many corporate settings. The places it is often found and sometimes tolerated, however, are highly creative jobs, like those in advertising and product design, for example. In jobs that require a high level of creativity, the organization is often willing to make allowances for an executive's lack of rationality if he can produce creative ideas. Particularly in advertising, irrational, highly emotional, and tantrum-driven behavior is considered the privilege of the successful advertising executive.

C A S E
S T U D Y

MANAGING UNDIFFERENTIATED PARENT AND THE CHILD EGO STATES

Ravi is an expert financial analyst. His specialty is savings and loan institutions, and he is a whiz at predicting which of these institutions is likely to make money and which will fail. He warned of the savings and loan disaster in the late 1980s before it happened, saving his client investors millions of dollars. Since then, his advice has always been right on the money. Ravi regularly golfs with the major CEOs in the industry and is consulted weekly by *Barron's, The Wall Street Journal*, and other fine investment publications.

There is no doubt that Ravi is brilliant and highly creative. His expert predictions about the savings and loan industry required far more than just intelligence—he relies equally on his "gut intuitions," which sometimes push him to defy logic and advise against the obvious trends in the numbers.

At work and at home, Ravi is a tyrant. He sees himself as a genius at financial issues and has absolutely no patience for anyone else in his field. When on the phone with other analysts or working with junior analysts in the office, he blows up at the slightest offense and spares no rage in dressing down the other person. At home, Ravi has been through three marriages, all but the third having ended in messy divorces. His current marriage isn't a happy one, and Ravi tries to spend as much time as possible away from home.

Ravi is a good example of an undifferentiated executive. Although he is exceptionally bright and talented, he often acts irrationally (intelligence has little to do with rational behavior—brilliant people act irrationally as often as everyone else). If you were to see him in action, you would immediately notice that he switches from his Parent (authoritative and sometimes punitive reactions to those he perceives as inferior to himself) and his Child (yelling laced

85

with vulgar language and intolerance for other's feelings). Even though he makes smart decisions, emotionally his Adult is relatively undeveloped. Given his financial wizardry, his superiors and colleagues give him permission to continue acting in this way, providing him with little incentive to change.

What brought Ravi to coaching was the midlife realization that his marriages had all ended in disaster; furthermore, he didn't have one person he really counted as a friend. This realization left him incredibly distraught, and although he wasn't yet willing to own the complete spectrum of his behavior at work, he had an idea that maybe something was wrong with the way he treated other people. This idea was, of course, fleeting, and much of the first weeks of coaching focused on bringing that idea back and dealing with it consciously.

Like Ravi, the undifferentiated executive is often very bright and highly creative. He trades on these attributes and believes that he has a right to act both parentally and childish because of his talents. Coaching can be of great value to the undifferentiated executive once he finds himself in crisis. This usually doesn't happen until midcareer and is often triggered by an unexpected failure or a feeling of alienation from other people.

The Coaching Process

Up to this point we've looked at the various aspects of coaching and the executive ego. Now, it's time to pull these pieces together into a cohesive coaching process. I've divided this process into four distinct phases:

1. Decontamination
2. Identifying the script, crisis, and associated fear complex

3. Identifying the triggers and alternative Adult behaviors

4. Homework

Decontamination

Decontamination is a term used in transactional analysis (TA) to describe methods of helping the client to consciously realize what is contained in each of his three ego states. It can be accomplished several ways, all of which are a variation of asking the same three simple questions:

❖ What does your Parent say about this situation?

❖ What does your Child say about this situation?

❖ What does your Adult say about this situation?

As simple as those questions are, they can be profoundly insightful for the client. Let me tell you a story about how it happened for one executive client whom I'll call Dale:

C A S E
S T U D Y

ENGAGING THE ADULT TO OVERPOWER THE IMPULSES OF THE CHILD

Dale was the president and CEO of a chain of forty restaurants. He had helped found the chain with two other partners fifteen years earlier. The company had been profitable for most of its history but was now seeing declines in revenue thought to be in part due to aging facilities and competition from new "concept" restaurant chains.

Dale went for coaching after a series of blowups he had with some of his long-term associates. Two had walked off the job and others, he was certain, were actively looking for other positions. Dale knew he was largely responsible for the turnover, but just couldn't seem to contain himself these days. Before coming to his session, Dale had just learned that one of his partners had hired an attorney and was demanding to be bought out. Cash was short at the moment, and Dale wasn't certain what to do. Unfortunately, his first reaction had been an outburst of anger that had served to only further alienate the partner.

When Dale sat in his coach's office and recounted these events, the coach began the process of decontaminating. It went something like this:

Coach: Dale, let's try to look at this objectively, okay? Let's start by looking at how you feel about it.

Dale: There's no doubt about how I feel. I'm damn angry!

Coach: It might be helpful in our work to separate each of your ego states on this issue. Let me start by asking you what your Child feels about it.

Dale (pause):   I'm angry and, I guess you could say, hurt by what John is doing. He knows this is the absolute worst time to demand a buyout. We've been through so much together and it's beyond me why he's doing this to me now.

Coach: Is it fair to say that your Child is hurt and feeling somewhat abandoned by a trusted friend?

Dale: I suppose . . . I feel like he lied to me about his commitment to this business.

Coach: All right, now how does your Parent feel about this?

Dale: John shouldn't be doing this right now. Our agreement was that we would never do anything to jeopardize the company. Buying him out now will most likely bankrupt us. I feel like he's breaking the rules.

Coach: So he's violating an agreement between the two of you. Was this agreement written, verbal, or just understood?

Dale: Mostly understood, I suppose. We did talk about it years ago when we first started, but it hasn't been an issue until now.

Coach: Do you have a written partnership agreement?

Dale: Yes, we signed it when we opened the first restaurant fifteen years ago.

Coach: What does it say about buyouts of a partner?

Dale (pause):   It states that if any one of the three partners wants out, he must request it in writing. The other two partners have twelve months to buy him out or all the assets of the partnership must be liquidated and distributed equally among the partners and the partnership will be dissolved.

Coach: Has John complied with this?

Dale: I think I see where you're going with this, and yes, he has complied.

Coach: So what do you think is the issue here?

Dale: I think I feel hurt and angry at John right now. But I'm also starting to see that he hasn't done anything wrong. I guess I may not like it, but he's perfectly within his right to do it.

Coach: Do you think John would be open to a compromise arrangement, like a buyout spread over two years?

Dale: Maybe. I was too angry at the time to ask.

The process of decontaminating this situation for Dale proved to be very insightful. He was seeing that it was his out-of-control Child that was causing him to act out. As Dale and his coach discussed it, the coach began to appeal to his Adult (e.g., "Do you have a written agreement?"). By engaging his Adult, he could recognize the impulses of the Child. That didn't make him feel less hurt or angry about the situation, but it did allow him to gain control over his behavior.

With Dale and other clients, this process of decontamination must be repeated time and again. We all learn best through repetitive action, so continually decontaminating problem situations teaches the client to recognize when he is acting out of his Parent or Child. That knowledge is often enough to help an executive gain control and insight into his feelings in order to to stop reacting in the same, detrimental manner. During the decontamination phase, it can be helpful to the coach to mentally map out the client's ego states. Understanding which state is usually dominant in stressful or problem situations can be very helpful in directing your work with client.

Identifying the Script, Crisis, and Associated Fear Complex

The next phase of coaching involves helping the client to identify the crisis he is experiencing. Part of that process also includes identifying the life script that has led up to the crisis and also identifying the fear complex that keeps him locked into his crisis. The process of identifying a crisis is the most complex component of coaching and consequently, requires more in-depth information. Part Three of this book will be devoted entirely to discussing each crisis along with the associated script and fear complex.

Identifying the Triggers and Alternative Adult Behaviors

Once the client has grasped an understanding of his crisis and how it works, he is ready to begin discovering the triggers that cause him to behave in ways that are non-Adult and keep him in crisis.

After more than a dozen sessions, Dale began to see that one of the biggest triggers for him was other people disagreeing with him. As soon as someone else criticized or even made a kind rebuttal to something he said or decided, he could feel himself slipping into a Child rage. He felt vague feelings of abandonment and fear. In our work together, he realized this was part of a larger life script that had begun in his childhood. Dale was raised by a strict and emotionally distant father who expected him to excel and punished him when he didn't. Furthermore, he was small for his age and was often bullied by the other boys during early school years. Ever since then, Dale had felt a strong obligation to always be perfect. And when he wasn't, he knew there'd be hell to pay at home.

Disagreements and conflict triggered these frightened feelings in Dale. It was as if he were suddenly expecting a blow from his father's belt, or maybe an encounter with a bully's fist after school. In defiance, he would strike back, trying to mollify these feelings and regain his emotional equilibrium. Hence, he reacted with outbursts of anger.

In recent years, Dale had begun to feel like more of failure. This activated those Child feelings of fear and dread that he had experienced in childhood. Slowly he had watched his successful business begin to become less profitable. It was still profitable, mind you, just not *perfectly* profitable. He was on edge, and it didn't take much from an employee, partner, and sometimes even a customer to activate his rage.

Dale's primary trigger was conflict. From that point forward, we worked on how he could immediately identify conflict and engage his Adult instead of the automatic Child response he had before. The Adult response, he decided, was to always pause for at least a few minutes and seriously consider the merits of the person disagreeing with him. Together we worked on this behavior by reverse role-playing conflict where I would play him and he would play the role of the person disagreeing with him. From these exercises, he gained a comfort level with first seeing a conflict through the other person's eyes. While it didn't mean that he would necessarily change his position, it definitely meant that he reacted to the conflict differently than in the past. He now had choices. He could either try to satisfy the other person's concerns by showing him the benefits of his ideas, or he could change his position to accommodate the other person. In addition, he learned to intervene when his Child made him feel like accommodating others made him a failure, and reminded himself that true success in business is not perfection, but good negotiation with others.

One useful tool for identifying a client's triggers is to have the client recount in detail what happened before and after the undesirable behavior occurred. Sometimes it takes two or three times before the trend emerges and triggers are identified. With some clients it can be helpful to have them close their eyes and do an imaginary walk through the situation. Such guided imagery can reveal details that otherwise might elude the client.

Homework

The final phase of coaching involves homework, or the assignment to practice what you've worked on during your session during the time between sessions. For example, if you are in the decontamination phase, have the client work during the week to analyze situations he encounters from all three ego states. If you are in the phase of identifying triggers, have the client return to the next session with at least one attempt to identify a trigger and alter his subsequent behavior.

Homework assignments should always be clear and specific. Furthermore, the coach should hold the client responsible for completing the previous week's assignment at each session. For most assignments, the homework is merely a self-report of the executive's experience; others assignments may involve writing or "journaling" his experiences.

EIGHT

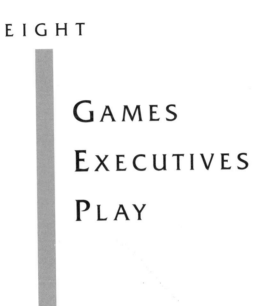

GAMES

EXECUTIVES

PLAY

Executives, like everyone else, sometimes play games to get their needs met when they feel that more direct methods may fail or be met with resistance. When they crave stimulation (e.g., new projects, change of scenery, and so on), recognition (e.g., a promotion, a bonus, attention from the CEO), or structure (e.g., power to set the agenda, familiarity in unfamil-

93

iar circumstances) but feel that more conventional methods won't work, such as working hard or interviewing for a new position, they resort to game playing.

In this chapter, I list some of the games I've seen executives play. Doubtless, you could add to this list from your own experience. The point of this chapter is not that you read each game and learn it specifically, but that you move through it quickly, spending more time on the games that are unfamiliar to you. As you begin your coaching practice, you'll find this chapter immensely helpful as a reference during those times of frustration when you and your client seem to hit an invisible wall. Most often, this happens because the client is invested in a particular game and is avoiding your attempts to move forward. By helping the client to acknowledge the game and its payoff, he can begin to free himself from the constraints of the game.

Games are closely tied to scripts, as described in Chapter Five. One important way that can help a client free himself from a script is by first acknowledging and disengaging from familiar games. Once he no longer chooses to play the game, the payoff stops and he must shift his time and energy toward other, more authentic, and efficient ways of getting his needs met.

Some games are often tied to specific scripts and crises. Other games may be a component in any number of crises. The better you as a coach become at recognizing and "calling" a game when it surfaces, the more effective you become. As long as a client remains bound in his games, he cannot break free from the script that is controlling him.

There are two excellent sources for more in-depth information on games: *Territorial Games* (New York: AMACOM, 1998) by Annette Simmons and *Games People Play* (New York: Ballantine Books, reprinted 1996) by Eric Berne.

Ain't It Awful

This game is played between the executive and a collective "they," most often senior management. It is played by blaming "them" for all the problems the executive experiences in his job. Usually the faultfinding is generalized and is not associated with a constructive attempt to fix the problem. Instead, the executive portrays himself as helpless. "They" are described as generally negligent, stupid, or too arrogant to care.

The payoff of this game is that the executive excuses himself from responsibility for solving problems by blaming others for them. This game can have additional payoffs if played among others who are disgruntled because they give their approval to the executive for playing their game.

This game is often coupled with a similar game: "Nowadays." This version of the game holds that everything in the present is inferior to what used to be. After an organizational restructuring or downsizing, you'll find many executives and employees playing this game.

The naïve coach will enter into this game in one of two ways: by suggesting ways of improving the situation (which is likely to be met with proclamations of why the coach's suggestions won't work) or by playing along and supporting the "blamescaping." Sometimes executives can be so convincing that the coach may believe that the situation really is miserable and unchanging. To test whether this is true, ask the executive what he has done to improve the situation. If he can't come up with anything substantial, he's playing the game. If he has made an honest effort to create positive change, then perhaps the situation is unworkable and a job change is in order.

In the final analysis, it isn't productive to remain in a miserable situation. The executive must decide whether he wants to create a solution or get out. Either way, he is taking positive action, but to continue playing "Ain't It Awful" is unproductive for both the executive and the organization.

Blemish

The game of Blemish is played when an executive continually exerts his superiority by always pointing out the minor errors of employees and colleagues. For example, after reviewing a very well researched and written report on a project that took six months to put together, he might comment, "Good report! There are two spelling errors that need to be corrected." Of course, it's not that spelling errors shouldn't be corrected, it's that they are probably a minor concern given the nature of the report.

The executive who plays this game is always on the look-out for infuriatingly insignificant details. He often misses the primary point because he is so focused on correcting small errors. Here's an example:

> One nonprofit executive, Peter, loved to play the game. Whenever one of his staff would write a grant proposal, Peter would closely edit it for any minor spelling or grammatical errors. Rarely would he make substantive changes to the content. Empowered by his blemish hunt, Peter would often exclaim how he was the only one who could write a decent grant proposal, despite the fact that his grant proposals were denied more frequently than those of his staff members. Peter used the game as a crutch to his waning self-confidence and to negate the threat he felt from his competent staff of employees.

Camp Out

This one's a territorial game where the executive stakes out a territory and then guards it carefully, despite what is best for business. This executive relies on a sense of ownership for his self-worth and, consequently, is extremely concerned about the part of the business he owns.

Remember the childhood game of musical chairs? In this game, there is always one fewer chair than people, so when the music stops, each person must scramble so as not to be the one without a chair. This is exactly how the executive playing Camp Out feels. He imagines that the pie just isn't big enough for everyone to be served a slice, so he must dive in and get his slice first.

The executive who plays this game is like the miser who stays up at night to count and recount his money. The number of employees, size of the budget, and organizational titles, these are all *very* important to him. He carefully monitors what other executives "own" and is mindful of any differences.

The payoff of this game is the boost the executive feels when he counts his organizational "possessions." The more he acquires, the better the high he feels when he counts it.

Cook the Books

The game of Cook the Books is played by the executive who, like a bad scientist, ignores contrary evidence and only presents information that supports his point of view. He manipulates others by giving them only data that will lead them to them to the conclusion that he has preordained. This game is more about one executive manipulating another than it is about good business judgment. In fact, the harder it is played, the more detrimental it can be to the business.

The payoff is that one executive is able to control others through his manipulation of information. He feels powerful when he does this and it temporarily contradicts his internal sense of powerlessness.

Various methods are common in this game, among them withholding key information, hiding or destroying negative information, and artificially manufacturing positive information. This game has a distinctive addictive quality to it, and once an executive successfully plays it, he often continues playing until caught.

One of the most public examples of Cook the Books was played by the former CEO of Sunbeam Corp., Al "Chainsaw" Dunlap. Eager to make Sunbeam look attractive to shareholders, Dunlap employed a number of techniques, including prebooking orders and relabeling old products as new ones. The result was that Sunbeam's books looked much better than they were in reality. Dunlap continued playing Cook the Books during his three-year tenure at Sunbeam until accounting officials exposed the game and Dunlap was fired.

Interestingly enough, there is strong evidence that Sunbeam was not the first organization where Dunlap played this game. It was his earlier activities as CEO of Scott Paper that caused government regulators to begin looking at what he was doing at Sunbeam.

At the time of this writing, Enron Corporation's former CEO Kenneth Lay has become the most notorious player of Cook the Books. Enron was a Wall Street darling until just a few months prior to a rescue takeover by rival Dynergy Inc. The deal fell apart amid investor concerns about Enron's murky finances, resulting in Enron filing the largest bankruptcy case in history. Among other irregularities, the bankruptcy proceedings revealed that Enron maintained numerous questionable "off-ledger" partnerships that hid billions of dollars in debt from auditors. Thousands of Enron employees lost their jobs and much of their retirement savings in the collapse.

Ambush

The executive who waits until another executive is in a position where he can't say no to a request is playing the game of Ambush. For example, if one executive wants another executive to allow an employee to transfer into his department, he waits to make his request until the other executive is in a public meeting, say with the CEO present, where it would appear "unteamworthy" for him to refuse the request, regardless of how he really feels. The game of Ambush is all about putting another person in an awkward position in order to get what one wants.

Masters of the game learn how to withhold information until the perfect moment, then blindside a colleague with it in order to get what they want. Some executives consider this game simple business strategy, but the effect within an organization or team is quite negative. Others resent being ambushed and sometimes begin playing the game with the executive as retribution. The game often starts a painful and inefficient cycle of back-and-forth retaliation among executives.

The payoff for the executive playing Ambush is, like in Cook the Books, a feeling of power and control. By manipulating other executives, the executive can temporarily assuage his self-doubts and feel mighty. It is, however, only temporary. Ambush must be continually played in order to maintain the executive's ego strength.

Debtor

This is one of the subtler games that executives play. It is played by one executive putting himself in debt to another executive or to the company. For example, the executive may deliberately fail in order to put himself in position of "debt" to his boss. This feeling of debt gives him a strong sense of purpose and he comes charging back with excellent results. The game of debtor is played in cycles that alternate between debt and payback.

The game supplies "substitute motivation" for the executive who has no other motive. As long as he is in debt, he is motivated to get out; but once out of debt, his motivation is gone, and he must go back into debt to succeed.

There are many ways this game is played. You'll recognize this game in the executive who isn't happy unless he's fighting an uphill battle. Once on top, he's miserable. Here's an example:

> Horace was the sixty-year-old owner and chief executive officer of a rural utility company. The first years Horace was in the position, he worked hard to overcome a serious deficit the company had accumulated and to repair a seriously flawed sewage treatment plant. Once he had accomplished these goals and the utility become quite profitable, Horace sold it and bought a chain of supermarkets. Ultimately, Horace was forced to declare bankruptcy because the supermarket chain was too much of a challenge for him. In retrospect, Horace realized that his game of Debtor had ultimately destroyed his career and a lifetime of financial investments.

The game of Debtor can be seen at work in almost every corporation. Executives yearning for stimulation make risky decisions so that they feel motivated to succeed. They support risky products and projects, spend large sums of money on questionable causes, and put their careers on the line for remote possibilities just to give themselves a psychic kick in the pants.

Did I Say That?

Of all the games, this one can legitimately be called crazy making. Why? Because it involves undermining another person's sense of reality and memory. Commitments that are made in private between two executives are denied by one executive in public. Looking slightly confused and mostly perturbed, the executive might say: "Did I say that? I don't remember having said anything of the sort . . . ." The other executive is left looking like a fool, or worse, a liar.

The chameleon-like executive who relies on the game of *Did I Say That?* isn't likely to succeed for long before others catch on to his game. Until they do, however, the executive is infuriatingly able to manipulate others by doublespeak and changing his commitments to suit his needs.

To a lesser extent, an executive with a crisis of commitment will play this game. He slightly varies his presentations, depending on who is in the audience and what he believes they want to hear from him. On the occasion that this duplicity catches up with him, he denies having made the earlier commitment (it's one reason he doesn't like to put things in writing, such as e-mail, so there is no paper trail).

The payoff is the executive's ability to dodge commitment. By flexing and swerving, he can avoid being pinned down to actual results. On the surface, he appears engaged and productive, but in reality he is busy dodging commitment.

Friends in High Places

The executive who uses his connections with more senior executives, important customers, or industry leaders to manipulate others is playing this game. He can play this game by dropping the names of important people and mentioning that he, too, is "in the know." Here's an example:

> Juan was a young executive who had recently graduated from an Ivy League business school with an MBA. He was ambitious and eager to be recognized as a potential leader in the organization. His father, a well-known expert in the field of quality engineering, had groomed him since he was young to follow his very successful path into business.
>
> Now, Juan was on the verge of being fired from his third job. He just couldn't understand why—he

blamed his employers as being too backward and unable to take advantage of his strategic mind. His father was embarrassed because he had pulled strings to get Juan into fast-track positions at great companies. Juan was slowly becoming bitter and depressed.

I met Juan when I was being interviewed by the organization to run the department in which he worked. In my first meeting with Juan, he mentioned all the great names in the fields of organizational development and psychology in the first half-hour. He would say things like, "During my last conversation with Ed Lawler . . ." or "when I had dinner with Warren Buffet. . . ." Then he told me how often he had met with the president of the company and that it was just a matter of time before he would be reporting directly to the president. By the way, did I know his father?

Needless to say, I was put off by Juan during our first short meeting and had good hunch that most everyone who worked with him was, too. As I began to become more familiar with the company and Juan's history with it, I discovered that I was right. Juan had been with the company for just under two years, and had he not been the son of a friend of the CEO, he probably would have been fired a year and a half ago. The bottom line was this: Juan made lots of big promises about grand ideas, which he laced with references to his famous acquaintances. When it came time to deliver, Juan rarely came through with the goods.

The game of Friends in High Places works only as long as the protector (the friend in a high place) is willing to protect his lower-level comrade. When this happens, the game can be played for many years. Others recognize the game and, while they resent it, often respect the protection it affords the executive. Should the protector be removed from power, however, the executive quickly finds himself in trouble.

Harried

Harried is played by the executive who wishes to appear extremely busy and needed by others. This executive suffers from "stress envy"—silently wishing to be stressed so that he can prove to himself and others that he is valuable.

This game is played more than most people realize. I have yet to work with an organization where an executive has the courage to say that he doesn't work very hard and leaves the office everyday at five and takes all weekends off. That would sound as if he weren't very important, because all-important executives are usually overworked and stressed out. So the executive who needs to feel important privately ensures that his calendar is always booked weeks ahead and that he is constantly running from one meeting to another, or even one coast to the other.

A common strategy in the game is for the executive to take on unnecessary projects and involve himself in trivial details that can best be handled by someone else. By keeping a finger in every project, this executive appears to be highly responsible and overworked. In reality, he's creating a great deal of make-work for the sake of his own self-esteem.

A common component of the Harried game is the feeling that "I'm working harder than you, so you can't criticize me." It's intended to intimidate anyone who might try to expose the game for what it is—unnecessary busyness. The phrase "work smarter, not harder" is common way in which organizations try to debunk the game of Harried among executives. Nevertheless, executives playing this game are very often able to fend off criticism by portraying themselves as martyrs for the company who never have time for themselves. This trick can intimidate other executives who are easily made to feel guilty. Shouldn't they, too, be working long hours?

He's Great, But Did You Know?

This game brings to mind the old insult, "That suit looks better on you every year that you wear it." It's all about hiding criticisms, insults, and treachery underneath the cover of a pseudo compliment. In many organizations, it may not be considered good teamwork to openly criticize a colleague, so an executive wishing to undermine another's image might play this game. This game often involves conversations with themes such as: "Wasn't that project well designed? Too bad it cost so much..." or, "I think he's doing a great job in the current position, and we wouldn't want to hurt his track record by giving him too much responsibility, would we?"

This game is an attempt to spread negative information without seeming to be vicious or mean-spirited. It's always risky to communicate negative information, especially when it affects another person. Rather than own up to that risk, the game of He's Great, But Did You Know? is an attempt to avoid the possible backlash that can hurt the communicator of bad news.

I'm Only Trying to Help You

This clever game can be observed among all executives, but particularly among human resources executives. It is played when an executive recommends that another executive take a certain action. When that action doesn't accomplish the desired result, the other executive returns to complain about what has happened. The executive, rather than evaluate what he has recommended, turns the blame subtly on the other person by suggesting that perhaps he didn't carry out the recommendation effectively.

Why does this happen frequently with human resources and other staff executives? Because their areas of expertise are quite often soft and unproven. Much of what is recommended is often based on policy or trends in the management literature and not on hard evidence of efficacy. Therefore, rather than explore the shortcomings of his professional recommendations, the HR or other executive disavows responsibility by saying he was only trying to help.

This game is very similar to another variant that might be called "For Your Own Good." This is a parental game that is sometimes played by an executive on his subordinates. When the subordinate questions the recommendation, the executive shuts down the discussion by saying something along the lines of "it's for your own good." The subordinate is left feeling inferior and is compelled to carry out the recommendation, even if it goes against his better judgment.

If It Weren't for You

If It Weren't for You is a game that is most often played by an executive and his boss. The executive blames his failures or waning motivation on a lack of support from his boss. The executive talks about all the wonderful things he could accomplish if he only had a boss who "gets it" or was working for a more progressive organization.

This game is a serious attempt to escape the complex and difficult process of getting things done in an organization. Much of the work a successful executive does is eliciting the support he needs from his superiors and the organization at large. This can be an enormous task, which is why some avoid it by playing this game.

One of the most extreme examples I've encountered was with an executive who worked for the federal government. He worked for a particular agency that wasn't a favorite of the Republican party, so from 1980 until 1992 he excused himself from taking responsibility for his own poor performance by blaming the Republican administrations that were in power during those years and had cut funding to the agency. When the administration shifted to the Democrats in 1992, he was left without an excuse and eventually took early retirement rather than work harder.

Other ways executives play this game is by blaming corporate initiatives. They will use phrases like: "If it weren't for the reorganization" or "If this place wasn't so backward." While this game may be based on some portion of fact, it is about using the unfavorable reality to avoid having to do some unpleasant or difficult tasks.

If That's What You Want

This game is best described as malicious obedience—doing what you are told even though you know it will fail. This game is played by a subordinate executive who feels intimated or inferior to his boss. Rather than confronting the boss with information he has that suggests the boss may be wrong, he withholds and follows the boss's instructions completely.

I've often seen this game at work when an executive is hired from outside the company to manage an existing department. The employees in the department, a few of whom probably thought they should have been promoted into the position, passively resist the new executive by withholding critical information about the organization, its history, and the hidden power dynamics at play. When the new executive makes a request that the employees know will fail, they start playing If That's What You Want. The subordinate executives know they can't be held responsible for following their new boss's instructions, so they express their anger by playing a game where they are protected from official sanctions.

Staff executives are frequently the object of this game when it's played by resistant line executives in the following way: The staff executive makes a request of the line executive. The line executive resents the intrusion. Rather than communicate his dissatisfaction, the line executive follows the staff executive's request even though he knows it will fail. When it does fail, he reports this back to the staff executive with a sense of victory and an attitude of "I knew it wouldn't work."

Kick Me

Kick Me is a game that outwardly has the message of "don't kick me" but creates the irresistible urge in others to do it. At first glance, this game may appear to be borderline insanity, but on second glance you'll notice that it is played quite a lot in the corporate arena. Executives playing Kick Me complain about the difficulty of their jobs, but continue to place themselves in difficult or impossible situations. The executive usually creates a "poor me" identity that includes frequent complaints about how difficult his job is and how badly he is treated. When confronted, he will say that he has no choice in the matter and answer "yes, but . . ." to most suggestions for change. The fact is, his ego is supported by the fact that he is the patron of lost causes.

This executive occupies a strange and secure role in many corporate structures. While most other executives know that he hasn't accomplished much of value (since he's always tied up with impossible causes), he is kept around to be the receptacle of projects that no one else dares attempt. For example, when the CEO wants every manager trained in a particular program, the Kick Me executive takes it on. Not only are these kinds of projects time-consuming, they often cost a great deal and produce little to show for the effort. In the end, this executive racks up big bills with little tangible success.

Let's You and Him Fight

This game is all about deflecting attention from oneself. The game is played by one executive passing along information that causes conflict between two other executives. For example, when an executive's project is failing, he starts conflict between two colleagues to divert attention from his own problems.

Sometimes this game is played so that the executive can reenter the dispute as the hero and resolve the conflict for the two executives. This makes the executive appear to be the rescuer and may raise his stock with more senior executives.

Make My Day

Make My Day is the bravado of an executive who feels inferior but insists on compensating for it with an outward show of force. This game is played by inviting others to challenge you while quietly but firmly threatening retaliation.

Few corporate environments would tolerate an out-and-out version of this game, but most harbor more covert varieties of it. For example:

> An accounting executive found that his department spent more time and resources on tracking executive expense accounts than just about anything else. Repeated requests that executives submit better expense reports failed, so the accounting executive

convinced the company's auditing firm to insist that the company adopt extremely tedious expense reporting procedures. The result? Expenditures on expense accounts dropped dramatically—not because the previous expenses were not legitimate, but because the new policies made reporting those expenses not worth the time and effort.

Making something "not worth the effort" is the resulting threat of the Make My Day game. When an executive makes statements such as, "If you don't approve my request for another employee, I'll be forced to cut back on the services my department provides to you," or "If I can't get the resources of this project, then I'll be forced to cut the project I've already started for your department," he's making subtle underlying threats. The message is always clear: Do what I tell you or your life will become difficult.

Now I've Got You, You SOB

In this game of entrapment, the executive creates a situation where another executive is sure to fail. When the executive does fail, the other executive holds it over his head in order to get what he wants. This game might also be called "Now You Owe Me One," since the net effect is for one executive to put the other executive under an obligation.

Now I've Got You, You SOB, often entails creating relatively nonsensical rules—not for the good of the company or executive, but so rule-breakers can be caught and threatened. Practices such as 7:30 a.m. staff meetings can be the product of this game because they're intended to catch those who usually don't arrive at the office that early. Another example might be the human resources executive who sits by idly while another executive makes a job offer to a new employee, despite the fact that head count quotas are already exceeded. After the executive makes the offer, the human resources executive pounces on him, calling him on the carpet for policy violations.

This game is very often played when an executive wants to fire an employee but isn't willing to go through the long process of documenting performance infractions. Instead, he creates a situation where the employee is likely to make a critical mistake either through ignorance or carelessness. Either way, when the employee makes the critical mistake, the executive uses it as an excuse to fire the employee on the spot.

Silent Protest

Silent Protest is an infuriating game when you're the object. Playing the game requires an executive to publicly commit to certain actions that he never intends to follow through with. The careful executive who plays this game only does it when there is no way to document whether he's followed through. For example, an executive may agree to call an important customer that he has a personal and long-standing relationship with on behalf of another executive. He never places the call and reports later that he did call, but was unable to achieve favorable results. Other examples include an executive agreeing to cooperate with a corporatewide project, but when requests are made of his employees, they are always too busy to become involved.

Silent Protest is frequently played in organizations where teamwork is highly valued. In such corporate environments, it would not look good to turn down a request for cooperation, even when the executive doesn't want to cooperate. To handle this, the executive simply agrees to cooperate and then never does. He realizes that it would appear bad for some other executive to call him on the carpet, especially if there is no documentation of his uncooperative stance.

Try and Get Away with It

This is the favored game of the executive who always walks the line between right and wrong, legal and illegal. The object of this game is to get as much as you can without getting caught breaking the rules. This executive pushes the limits, often beyond where others are willing to go.

Examples include the real estate executive who outbids other buyers for a building, all the while knowing that he will drum up problems and request credits later that will reduce the cost of the building to below what the other bidders originally offered. Another example is the sales executive who promises employees enormous bonuses if sales reach certain, unattainable levels. The executive knows he can never pay such large bonuses and that it is highly unlikely that anyone will reach the goal, but he uses it as incentive to get as much work as possible out of his sales force.

This thrill game pays off for the executive who is hungry for the kind of stimulation that his job doesn't normally provide. It's no longer enough to do the job—he must push the rules as far as he can without getting caught. When he's successful at doing this, he gets a charge out of it. Typically, the game becomes addictive and continues until the executive actually crosses the line, which may ultimately result in the demise of his career.

Up in Arms

Up in Arms is played by the executive who makes such a big commotion whenever something happens that he dislikes, other executives learn to avoid crossing him. It just becomes easier not to offend this executive than to risk having a big scene played out in front of other executives.

The way in which this game is acted out is for the executive to play up transgressions in places where it might embarrass the "offending" executive. For example, in a meeting the game-playing executive may say, "Well, the last time you promised us resources, it never materialized, so I'm not sure that I believe what you're saying now." Thus, the other executive is made to look like a liar in front of colleagues. Any response this executive makes in self-defense is likely to make him look guilty and may only do more harm. He is caught and there's not much he can do about it. Rest assured, he won't let it happen again.

The tactics of this game require exaggeration and embarrassment. The executive must take perceived offenses and paint them to appear worse than they really were to embarrass the offending executive. Much like the child who throws a tantrum in the grocery store to embarrass his mother into giving him what he wants, the executive playing Up in Arms is seeking to get what he wants by affecting the impressions of others.

"Why Don't You, Yes But . . ."

You'll recognize the executive playing this game. He's the one who requests help, not in order to receive help, but to establish for himself and everyone else that he is in a helpless situation and cannot reasonably be held responsible for the results. The game is played when one executive offers a helpful suggestion to another executive who responds by saying "yes but . . . ." The game continues with one or more executives offering help, all of which are met with reasons why the suggestion won't work. Finally, everyone throws up their hands and concludes that situation is helpless.

Executives playing this games say things like: "Yes, but we tried that before and it didn't work then." Or they say, "Yes, but we're not that kind of company—it won't work here."

It is certainly legitimate to challenge a helpful suggestion, but all too often this game is being played when suggestion after suggestion is rebuffed. The truth is that few situations are truly helpless and there is almost always a solution, however difficult or costly it may be. This game is played not to solve the problem, but to protect the game player from having to embrace difficult solutions or to be responsible for failure.

Wooden Leg

It's really hard to attack a wounded man, and the executive who plays Wooden Leg uses this strategy to create a safe haven for himself. He takes an infirmity and uses it as a shield against criticism or challenge. When the infirmity is personal, such as having a disabled child or losing a spouse, the executive continually uses this tragedy long after it has occurred. He takes the opportunity to remind others of his infirmity—he may collect donations for the local school for disabled children or hold support groups in the lunchroom for grieving spouses. While all of these activities are truly wonderful endeavors, the game-playing executive uses them to his advantage. He gets as much mileage as possible out of others' sympathy and uses it as an excuse for poor performance without consequences. After all, who would fire him after he lost his wife (never mind that it was five years ago)?

Some executives play Wooden Leg by taking on projects that no one else wants but are necessary for the company. Maybe the project means managing the hopelessly out-of-date distribution center that will eventually be phased out, or taking on the sales of the company's loss-leader product line. Who will criticize this executive when he has been given such mundane and hopeless projects? This executive is in essence saying, "Don't expect me to keep up, I've got a wooden leg!"

PART THREE

THE RELATIONSHIP CRISES

This section describes the three most common crises that have a negative effect on an executive's business relationships. While each chapter describes a distinct crisis, in practice it is not uncommon to find elements of more than one crisis involved.

NINE

THE CRISIS OF INDIVIDUATION

That evening I got home and I was standing in the bedroom when it happened. Something in me snapped, and suddenly I knew I had been passed over for good: I knew I'd come to the end of the line. I needed help badly . . . .

Ever since I can remember, I've wanted one thing . . .

when I made it to a director position, I told myself that I had finally earned it. I was part of the company's inner circle. Throughout my career with the company I've been willing to do whatever it takes to move up the ladder. Some guys get caught up in the infighting and insist on forcing their will on the company. Not me. I go with the flow and try not to make waves. Not that I'm a slacker—I work hard and put in long days. It's more that I believe in being a team player. You might call me a company man, although that term has a really bad rap these days, but it's true about me. My loyalty has always been with the company. I'm proud to say that work for this company—it's all I've ever wanted to do.

I don't know exactly when it starting happening, but I first remember thinking that something was wrong when they didn't include me in the senior manager retreat. Of course, there were the usual excuses of limited space and the need to mentor some younger executives, but the message seemed clear to me: I wasn't cutting it in someone's eyes. It became harder for me to get face time with the CEO and my budget was slowly being diverted to other departments. Then came the news . . . I was being reassigned to "special projects." Everyone knows that's nothing more than a graveyard. What are "special projects," anyway?

After everything I've sacrificed for this company, it's come to this. I guess it's true . . . nobody cares about your career but you. I feel totally washed up. I'm too old and too proud to start at the bottom somewhere else—besides, I don't want to work somewhere else. I know this place inside out. I've paid my dues. I should be moving up, not out. Damn it, I deserve better than this.

Teamwork. Fitting into the corporate culture. Soliciting feedback. Involving stakeholders. Compromise. These are all good things, in moderation. When they become more important to an executive than just about anything else he does, that's when the trouble starts. This is the crisis of individuation.

The crisis of individuation happens when an executive derives too much ego strength from being part of a larger, more important group. At first, this need to find personal meaning by being part of a larger group looks like the ideal executive. He works hard to fit in and is sure to check in with all the right corporate players before making a big decision. People generally like him, and he seems to be the perfect company man.

This crisis is often triggered by a change in management staff or direction that requires the executive to make some painful and unpopular decisions, like discontinuing popular product lines, or reorganizing a close-knit department.

The executive with a latent crisis of individuation just isn't equipped to make these kinds of decisions. He wants everyone to like him, and he's confused about what to do now. The programs and processes that he sponsored and that were once highly valued may now be considered part of the organization's problem.

So what does he do? He freezes. His world has become a political minefield where only the savvy survive. He's not necessarily savvy, just loyal. He was rewarded for his loyalty in the past, so he continues with the same approach, and this only gets him into deeper trouble. Others start to see him as part of the "old guard" that must be changed. He is slowly transitioned out of the flow of critical communication and marginalized.

By the time he realizes what has happened to him, he's probably already shut out of the power channel that he once was in. He panics. He asks himself, "I haven't done anything different from what I've always done. Why is this happening?" He sees himself as a good guy who has been unfairly and brutally treated.

I Just Want to Belong to the Inner Circle

The executive who is experiencing the crisis of individuation feels duty-bound to the organization, but at the same time resents it, although he would never admit this openly. He is confused and hurt over the rejection he feels from his peers/superiors. He feels he's done nothing to deserve what is happening to him now and is probably clinging to fantasies about "the way things used to be around here." If events have progressed, he may have been given the strongest of signals from his superiors that he should leave the organization—perhaps he's even been told this directly—but he continues to stay with the organization and fails to start the process of finding another job.

All of this can manifest in either depression or in vocal opposition to the current management regime. He may seek to undermine certain aspects of the new changes by using his strong connections with people throughout the organization.

The core feeling here is the fear of abandonment. This executive has a strong need to belong to something bigger than himself, and he can't tolerate the idea of being rejected from it.

C A S E
S T U D Y

DETRIMENTAL DEDICATION

Sam founded one of the largest and most successful environmental advocacy organizations in the country. He took it from its beginnings as a brief discussion at his kitchen table to an organization with a professional staff of twenty. As executive director of the organization, he had brought the organization to national prominence and had successfully changed the foresting practices in most of the western states.

Sam admits that the organization was his life and that it took a heavy toll on his marriage and family. He was always working, traveling to a site where environmental damage was occurring, or protesting before some governmental agency. Being part of the organization made Sam feel part of something important, and he treasured the organization and his handpicked staff deeply.

More than ten years after founding the organization, a number of the professional staff and members of the board of directors began to question Sam's ability to lead the organization as executive director. They began talking to him about stepping down. At first he was agreeable, since being executive director of a growing organization took much of his time away from the advocacy work he loved and forced him to spend increasing amounts of time on administrative duties.

After some time, the organization hired a replacement executive director. Sam wanted to stay a part of the organization, and since he was the founder, no one on the board of directors was willing to suggest that it might be better that he leave.

For six months after the hiring of the new executive director, Sam continued with the organization, constantly involving himself in everything and regularly circumventing the new executive director. When the new executive director made a remark to the press that Sam didn't agree with, Sam immediately criticized the executive director and eventually wrote a letter to the board of directors (which was mostly composed of Sam's supportive friends and colleagues) suggesting that the executive director had made a grave mistake.

In frustration, the new executive director quit. Sam, still unaware of how his actions had adversely affected the organization, expected to take the helm again as executive director. But the board of directors thought otherwise. They saw how Sam's unrelenting need to be part of the organization prevented him from holding any position. No matter what position he held, he would interfere with management of the organization. No, they thought it best that Sam retire when another executive director was hired.

Sam's retirement party was a true love fest, with lots of stories and tears. Employees, colleagues, and volunteers loved Sam and visibly showed their appreciation for what he started. It was clear that Sam had done something very important in the environmental movement.

Two months after the retirement party, Sam founded a rival organization that would not only have the same mission, but would compete for the incredibly scarce funding available to environmental advocacy groups from large foundations. In effect, Sam was trying to recreate his success, regardless of what it did to the original organization.

The case of Sam is complex and layered, but it clearly shows what an unresolved crisis of individuation can push an executive to do. It's true that Sam was extraordinarily driven to accomplish something for the environment; but the dark side of that extreme determination was an insatiable need to feel love and acceptance from something bigger than himself. Sam was so driven that he created an organization to provide that for himself. When the time came for Sam to hand over the reins of the organization in order to take the work he had started to greater heights, he began acting in ways that were decidedly detrimental to the organization in an effort to preserve his position within it. His need to be part of something bigger eventually eclipsed his own passion for environmental advocacy.

Sam is quietly angry over what happened to him at the Environmental Guardians. How could the board have rejected him? After all he had done, how could they possibly tell him to leave the organization? He felt deeply betrayed by some of his closest friends, no less.

The Hero Who Stayed Too Long

Others are likely to view this executive in one of two ways: as someone who isn't willing to change, or as a hero who is protecting the essence of the organization. Take your pick—both responses are likely. Because he is so likable, a sizable minority of employees and mangers will support him and be angry that he has been removed from power.

In our case study of Sam, colleagues and associates respected him. He had accomplished environmental changes that no one else even imagined. No one doubted that Sam's name would be prominent in the history of the environmental movement in America. Yet many people also saw Sam as a problem. They knew he viewed the Environmental Guardians as "his" organization and that he needed to be calling the shots. Sam was a brilliant activist, but not such a great executive. Those who were close to Environmental Guardians and who felt deeply about its work—many of them close friends of Sam—privately applauded Sam's retirement.

Sam was so likable and inspiring that some of the volunteers and other members of the organization weren't pleased about what had happened to him. They felt a great loyalty to him and his accomplishments. After the dust settled, Sam quietly convinced some of them to leave the Environmental Guardians and join his new organization.

Too Many Irons in the Fire

The executive with a crisis of individuation often has difficulty sticking with one business strategy and executing it consistently. Because of his strong need to please everyone, he often changes, amends, and deviates from his stated plans and instead tries to do what will please others. The end result is that nothing he does significantly departs from the status quo.

This executive can also be fiercely protective of employees who are supportive of him, regardless of their productivity. He will retain those who are doing little more than occupying space if they demonstrate loyalty to him and his programs. Over time he may build quite an empire of strangely incompetent employees that has a "clubby" feel to it.

Conversely, this executive has little patience for new employees who espouse radical ideas or contradict the status quo too publicly. For him, it is very important that employees "fit into the culture" by not criticizing existing programs, procedures, and regulations, regardless of the merits of the criticism or the efficacy of the suggested change. When working for this executive, the quickest way to be fired is to be too critical of the status quo. Being a team player is extremely important to this executive, and this he requires of himself as well as those who work for him.

Pleasing Everyone Pleases No One

The crisis of individuation, if left unresolved, can cause an executive to lose the acceptance and approval he has worked so hard to achieve. One executive, whom I'll call Ken, tells in his own words how his unresolved crisis determined much of his life, including his two failed marriages and ultimately, his career derailment.

> I have guilt feelings about the break up of my first marriage and find it difficult to talk about. The strain began to take a toll on my wife fairly early. I was working long hours and late in my earlier job as an industrial relations assistant. You see, then I used to get about 450 grievances a week and this was a plant of about 6,000 people. I had secretaries on both shifts. I had six guys who investigated the grievances, but I personally wrote all the answers. That's also something I started in the first big corporation I went to—writing a grievance answer, which reviewed the case, the position of each of the parties, and then came to a conclusion—all in a report. This practice was ultimately adopted in that big company. But it took time, and at that point I hadn't learned to delegate. One of the things this fellow, who was a plant manager I worked for, taught me was how to delegate. It was painful, but I eventually learned. He was single and at five o'clock every night he'd walk by my office on the way home and he'd say: "Aren't you going home?" And I'd say: "You got to be crazy—who's going to write up all these grievances?" He'd answer: "There are people out there"— he'd point to the department—"who are just dying to help you, if you'd let them." The way I'd respond was . . . you know I'd never really say it . . . but what I meant was: "Hey, look, this is my big chance. How can I get the attention of upper management by giving the work to someone else? I want them to know that I did this myself."

Well, finally, of course, I couldn't do it all, and he was relentless. First, he'd chide me and finally he'd say: "Where is the work we talked about?" I'd say: "I didn't have the time." And he'd answer: "You know, Ken, we've got to get it done. I don't care whether you haven't the time. There'd be time if you'd delegate." So finally I learned the hard way. As I say, it was painful, but it was a lot better than sitting down and explaining why I couldn't do it. He brought that home to me loud and clear. During that period I'd come down at night and dictate and I was just never home. During that time we had two children a year apart, so that's when the strain began to show. Then we went down south for two years in that plant and finally back up to headquarters in New York, when my wife was in about her seventh month of pregnancy. We were in New York only a year and then I went to this other plant; there was no question about it, I was driven to be one of the company guys. Actually, the thing that motivated me most of all was not so much the success, but to become part of the executive level. I wanted to be part of that group more than anything. I suppose that comes from childhood, but security and acceptance have always been important to me.

Security and acceptance—that's what I've looked for. Conflict across the table with the union never bothers me—that's competition. But conflict with people I cared about has always bothered me. I'll compromise to the point where I'll get myself in trouble by compromising rather than face the issues, and I did that with my wife. I knew I was wrong and I made promises that I just knew intuitively I couldn't keep.

So when I remarried after we were divorced, I married my secretary because I thought surely she understood all these things. Well, she didn't and now she's gone, too . . . .

Ultimately Ken lost the affection and approval he spent most of his life trying to earn. By working to be all things to all people, he exceled at nothing and eventually found himself pulled into a cyclone of working harder to be liked than to make money. After twenty years with the company, he was fired. Fortunately for Ken, he was able to find help and is now well on his way to rebuilding his life and career.

Analysis Paralysis

One of the great criticisms of America's older high-technology companies is that they have a long history of being too short on action and much too long on analysis. Having worked for one of those great companies early in my career, I can say it was once true. It seemed to be a corporate culture sort of thing—you had to involve everyone and get everyone's "buy in" before you proceeded with any new project. Sometimes it took years to get everyone to agree on something, and by that time, the need for the project had passed or morphed into something very different.

The executive who suffers from an unresolved crisis of individuation can sometimes find himself in "analysis paralysis." Analyzing a problem doesn't offend anyone; it usually doesn't step on anyone's toes or cross over into their prized territory. Taking action, on the other hand, has a high potential for offense somewhere in the organization. The bigger the action, the more likely you will transgress someone's territory or agenda adversely. It's just a rule of the corporation.

CASE STUDY

THE FRAZZLED AND PARALYZED EXECUTIVE

Carolyn was thorough in everything she did. No detail was ever left unattended. Her latest project, one that no one else in the company wanted to touch, she embraced with the same vigor and focus she was known for. Granted, revising the company performance evaluation system wasn't the most glamorous job, but it gave her opportunity and the reason to meet with top executives. What better visibility could she get in an otherwise lowly human resources job?

Carolyn mapped out her strategy. First she would hold discussion groups in every department and at every level to see what the needs might be. Once she compiled her needs assessment, she would present it to her superiors and to company management. From there, she'd hire a consultant to design an evaluation form that could be used companywide. After the first draft was complete and approved by her superiors, she would present it to focus groups across the country. Once all the feedback from the focus groups was incorporated into the form, she'd present it to her superiors and to company management. If they had no further changes, she'd begin the process of training managers to use the new form to evaluate their employees.

Somewhere in between the discussion groups, the executive feedback, and the focus groups Carolyn was buried underneath a virtual mountain of feedback forms, alternate drafts, and group discussion notes. One department needed the evaluation form to look one way, while another wanted something quite the opposite. The senior executives wanted a five-point rating scale, and the CEO thought a succinct three-point scale would be simpler and more appropriate.

Carolyn was torn, frazzled, and paralyzed. No matter how she altered the form—and she'd altered it no less than a few hundred times—someone had a big problem. Someone's ideas were always left out, no matter what she did.

Time dragged on, and after a year and a half Carolyn had little more than what she started with. She kept trying to get everyone's agreement, but was never completely successful. In the meantime, the senior executive team began to complain to the vice president of human resources, Carolyn's boss's boss, that human resources hadn't produced the promised performance evaluation form and process.

Carolyn's story is a good example of what happens to an executive caught in the crisis of individuation. The more she tries to solicit the ideas of those whose approval she wants, the more she must compromise her work. Eventually, whatever the project might be becomes a project "designed by committee" and doomed to failure. The project includes some portion of everyone's ideas, but in the end—if there is an end—it isn't useful to anyone.

"Churning feedback" is a common symptom of executives caught in the crisis of individuation. They solicit and process feedback from all the right people, but never seem able to produce something useful. At times, whole departments can be consumed by one executive's crisis of individuation, with each employee's time occupied with trying to win the approval of others in the organization.

Building a Helping Relationship

Coaching the executive who is experiencing the crisis of individuation requires a strong relationship between the coach and the client. This crisis touches on some very vulnerable feelings within the client, so the coach can help only after a strong relationship has been established.

Building a strong relationship from the beginning requires two things. First, the coach should never try to move faster than the client is truly ready to go. Second, the coach must spend time getting to know the client *through the client's eyes.*

Getting to know a client through his eyes means you must understand the client's world as he sees it—not as you might see it. What does the client see as his biggest challenges? What successes is he most proud of? How does he see his relationships? What is he most passionate about? How does he view his crisis? What does he think is the answer to his dilemma?

In short, you've got to see his world as he experiences it. Furthermore, he must know that you understand his world before he begins to trust you.

Building this kind of relationship is never simple or straightforward. Every client relationship is different. Let me give you example of how I worked to establish a strong relationship with a client who was experiencing the crisis of individuation.

CASE STUDY

LEARN AND LISTEN, AND COACH WITHOUT JUDGMENT

Charles was a vice president in charge of distribution at a national retail grocery business. He supervised four enormous distribution centers (each covered the square footage of five football fields) located strategically across the country so that no store was more than one day's drive from a distribution center.

If ever there was a "good old boy" executive, Charles was it. He had risen through the union ranks at the southwest distribution center and had eventually transferred to corporate headquarters in Florida. Everyone generally liked Charles, and although he only attended two years of college, he was clearly very smart and knew the distribution process of the grocery business better than anyone.

Although the corporate headquarters crowd seemed to like Charles well enough, he was never really welcomed into the inner circle of power by his fellow vice presidents. When serious issues of marketing strategy or store expansion arose, he was left out of the decision-making process.

When I first met Charles, I remember thinking how uncomfortable he seemed to be in the corporate uniform of suit and tie. The clothes just didn't seem to match his demeanor, and he seemed restrained by them. Whenever we met at the end of the day, Charles would have shed the coat and tie, rolled up his sleeves, and his once-pressed shirt would appear so disheveled that you might have thought he had slept in it the night before.

The fact that Charles knew the company's distribution process better than anyone else was, in the end, the triggering event for his crisis. The time had come to modernize and computerize the extremely complex process of receiving shipments of produce, meats, dairy products, beverages,

127

frozen foods, and household supplies from vendors, process-ing all of it, and then shipping just the right amount to each store.

Distribution in the grocery business is particularly difficult, since all the produce, meats, and dairy products have a lim-ited shelf life. You can't receive a large shipment and allow it to sit around a warehouse until the stores can handle it. No, you've got to plan exactly how much will be needed in each store, receive only that amount from your vendors, and then have the trucks ready to ship it to your stores. Furthermore, you try not to send out a truck unless it is completely full.

Charles knew these problems intimately and had spent his entire career solving them—without relying too much on computers. Now he was being told to modernize each distri-bution center with computerized conveyor belts and elec-tronic sorting equipment, eliminating the need for hundreds of personnel who had done this work manually in the past. Everything about distribution would have to change, and Charles would be forced to make some difficult, if not dis-tressing, decisions.

Charles felt completely trapped. He was trapped between a corporate office that was pushing for greater efficiency with computerization and four distribution centers that ran like clockwork without it. Few of his employees at the distribu-tion centers understood the concept of computerization, much less the highly technical knowledge necessary to run the computers. They complained bitterly to Charles; after all, they had increased their throughput each year for the past five years. Wasn't that good enough? Couldn't Charles do something about these corporate types who had never even visited a distribution center, much less worked in one?

Charles wanted to please them all. Unfortunately, he was in a situation where he had to make some choices if he wanted to survive in his position. He was frozen with anxiety. He knew the staff at each distribution center well and was friends with many of his managers, with whom he had worked for more than a decade and a half. They were all upset and complaining to him about the changes. They were certain computerization would fail and end up costing the company far more than the current manual system. What's more, their jobs were on the line and they knew it. They were looking to Charles to protect them.

This was the situation when I met Charles. He was skeptical from the very beginning about our work together. He had more than he could handle on his plate right now—why did he need to waste an hour a week with a coach?

We spent the first sessions together discussing Charles's job. Without judgment or advice, I tried to listen as carefully as I could, trying to reflect back to Charles my understanding of his situation. I didn't push and allowed Charles to talk about whatever he wanted to talk about, even if it seemed unimportant to our work together. Eventually, I noticed Charles began to relax and enjoy our sessions. He began to open up more and talk about his personal thoughts and feelings. It wasn't until we met a half dozen times that Charles and I were ready to really begin the work of coaching.

From that point forward, Charles and I were able to work more honestly than I would have thought possible after our first session. At that time, it was clear that he viewed me as just another corporate consultant who would take his time and not offer much in return. After he began to trust me, things changed. He began to open up and talk about himself and his work in a way he hadn't been able to with me before. In time, we were able to make some great progress toward resolving his crisis.

While it may seem like insignificant or a waste of coaching sessions, spending the time—even several entire sessions—to really get to know your client is very important. The secret to building a trusting relationship with a client lies in your intuition. No one can teach you how or what to do. It's something of an art, and you've got to feel your way through it. What's happening for your client right now? Does he trust you enough to be completely honest with you? What can you do to show the client that you really understand the issues he faces and that you can be of practical help to him?

The Fear Complex

The heart of this crisis is the fear complex of abandonment. The fear of abandonment comes from the Child fearing that he will be left to fend for himself, an impossibility in his infantile state. To mollify this fear, he unconsciously attempts to win the approval of everyone he encounters.

The coach's job is to create an environment with the client where he can begin to talk about his overwhelming need to be liked by others and how this need has affected his life. You must provide careful feedback and ask probing questions without being judgmental or condemning. Examples of statements you might use include:

"Why is it important that everyone approve of your decision?" "How does it feel to you to make difficult decisions?"

"Why does it feel that way?"

"How has the need approval affected your relationships throughout your life?"

As you begin to gently probe, you'll discover that the client will teach you a great deal about the fear of abandonment and how it has affected his life. He knows better than anyone the driving compulsion and nearly impossible expectations it puts on him to please everyone. He knows the anxiety that keeps him up at night, worrying that someone might be upset with something he's done and how it tortures him day and night.

The new executive coach is often tempted to *tell* the client what he is feeling, rather than *listening* to the client tell him what he is feeling. The client is telling you what he is feeling if you only have the ears to hear it. You simply act as a mirror and a magnifier, reflecting back what he tells you he feels.

CASE STUDY

HOW FEAR CAN RUN AN EXECUTIVE'S LIFE

John was the director of research and development for a small electronics firm. John consistently blamed the marketing department for the problems he was experiencing:

John: Marketing consistently promises far more than we can design into a box. I've worked here for ten years and have yet to see them honestly represent a product in development.

Coach: It must be frustrating trying to please them.

John: You bet it is. If I don't find a way to include all the features they've promised, then I've not only got angry customers, I have to answer to upper management as to why the product didn't "meet expectations." But who set the expectations? Not me!

Coach: So you feel trapped between marketing and upper management. Is that accurate?

John: You better believe it. And not only that—I've got a whole department of headstrong engineers to manage. Do you have any idea how hard it is to go back to those engineers and tell them to redesign a box with more features? I can tell you, it's sheer hell.

What John is telling the coach is that he is exasperated from trying to please every one—the marketing department, upper management, and his own employees. He'll never be able to do it—that's a given—but he continues to hold himself to this impossible standard. Why? What makes him want to continue to be all things to all people? Why is he willing to wreck his own sanity just to please others?

It's easy to want to fix John's problem for him at this point. If you've worked with organizational processes like I have,

131

you probably want to dive into the information flow and process between John's department and marketing. Where is the feedback loop to the engineers from the sales force? Are there focus groups of customers involved early in the design phase? What is the communication process with upper management? How can John manage upward better?

If this was your first reaction too, hold on. Those are the questions of an astute consultant, not an executive coach. You aren't here to fix the situation, or for that matter, to fix John. You're here to help John fix his own situation.

The core problem here is John's crisis of individuation, not the triggering event of this problematic situation with marketing. The problem is clear: John wants to please everyone. *And it is impossible.* The problem isn't the triggering event; it is John's crisis.

Rather than dissect and correct the organizational issues, you want to help John look at why he's in the situation and how he got here. There's no doubt that John is quite capable of charting the flow of information between his department and marketing to correct the situation, but for some reason he hasn't done this. Why hasn't he?

John's overwhelming need for approval from everyone has backed him into a corner. Any way he turns, he's bound to cross-purposes with someone, and that is something he can't bear to do. He's bright and motivated and spends all his energy trying to figure out the single path that will make everyone happy and also get the job done.

As John's coach, you'll work with him to explore these issues. Can anyone, in any job, really expect to please everyone? Of course not, but John doesn't believe this. Despite tons of contrary evidence in his own career, he slogs away, trying to do the impossible.

John is deeply afraid of abandonment. To put it another way, he's afraid that if he disappoints others they will no longer like him. If they don't like him, he'll fail, because he knows he's dependent on others for success.

For this executive, it can be quite helpful to talk about where this powerful fear of abandonment comes from. As an infant he was helpless and dependent on his caregivers for everything. If his caregivers abandoned him, he would die. That fear progressed through childhood, most likely from a feeling of instability or conditional love from his parents.

This primal fear can continue throughout an executive's life, leaving him victim to the feeling that he must please others in order to avoid their wrath. Deep inside, he believes that his survival depends upon winning and keeping the approval of others.

John's fear of the disapproval of marketing is somehow linked to this basic fear. He's overwhelmed with an anxiety, but he doesn't know consciously the root of his fear. He just knows that he *must* win approval.

Understanding the Life Script

The insight that will help John, from our previous case study, and all other executives struggling with a crisis of individuation is this: Most of the important decisions of their lives and careers have been based on winning the approval of others.

This insight, when achieved by the client, is hugely effective in moving toward crisis resolution. The realization that his life is the cumulative effect of a life script about trying to meet other people's expectations of him is both disturbing and challenging. If he hasn't seen himself this way before, it will make him feel as if he has abandoned himself and his own dreams for most his life.

The coach's job is to help the client deal constructively with this insight into his life script. There are several sensitive areas here that the coach needs to be careful about when exploring this insight. The first problem area is when the client achieves this insight and then proclaims himself a new man. This is often a way of avoiding dealing with insight—to simply assume that because you have discovered the problem, the problem is therefore solved. But it isn't.

Insight is just one of the beginning steps in resolving the crisis, and it won't bring about resolution unless it is carefully followed with specific behaviors. In other words, the client has to begin the hard work of practicing what he has discovered, and that is the hardest part of all. As Freud often noted, "Insight is not necessarily change."

Another potential problem is that the client has become so good at meeting other people's expectations that he probably doesn't have the skills to moderate his own behavior. For example, he may decide that he is going to do things his way from now on and, consequently, infuriate everyone with whom he works. Why? Because he doesn't have the finessing skills required to choose which expectations he will meet, he swings in the complete and opposite direction of not trying to meet anyone else's expectations.

That causes problems on three fronts. First, corporate life requires all of us to determine which expectations of us are critical, and then we must act to meet those expectations. When choosing which expectations to meet, you better be able to determine which ones are critical, or you'll quickly find yourself out of a job. This client has very poor skills in selecting critical expectations and will need coaching to help him understand which ones he must meet and which ones he might choose not to meet.

The second problem it causes is that other people are accustomed to him eagerly accepting and meeting their expectations. That's the person he's been, and when he suddenly stops doing it, it angers people. For example, when an executive is known to be particularly hard-driving and proprietary, other people don't expect him to quickly meet their expectations. They know they must "sell" him on the idea first, and then maybe he'll commit. On the other hand, the executive who has always been an "easy sell" and who suddenly refuses to respond that way any more becomes an enigma to others, frustrating and confusing them. Suddenly, other people don't know how to respond to him.

Finally, the third problem is that this executive doesn't have experience in saying no. There is an art to saying no gracefully, without alienating the other person. Many executives learn this skill early in their careers as a means of turning down all but the most important and focused of tasks. This executive has little experience in editing down his to-do list and will have difficulty telling others that he can't do what they are asking him to do. Here again, the coach can offer some solid help on how to be assertive while politely turning down requests that aren't critical.

This crisis may also be closely linked to another of the motivation crises, the crisis of passion. Since he has spent most of his career catering to the expectations of the powerful, he may have lost touch with his own passion, interests, and dreams. He may not have a clue what he really wants out of his career other than the next higher position and a bigger paycheck. Of course, those things will never satisfy and will only lead to a greater hunger for power and money, but the executive can't see that now. Most of his life has been spent chasing the expectations of others. As his coach, you've got to be the "training wheels" that help him discover, practice, and grow stronger in following his internal career compass.

Finding the Courage

Once the client has uncovered his fear of abandonment and recognizes his long-standing pattern of winning the approval of others at all costs, the next stage of coaching is to help him find the courage to follow his own convictions, regardless of how it may appear to others.

The ultimate task of the coach is to help client find courage within himself to overcome the present obstacle. No matter what the crisis, courage is the final goal of the coaching process. Once the client discovers that he has the courage within himself to resolve the crisis rather than continuing to avoid it, he is equipped to move himself and his career forward.

In the crisis of individuation, the client lacks the courage to stand up for what he believes is true. To date, he's made a successful career out of discovering what powerful others believe is true for him, and then following that "truth" wherever it leads him. The thought of standing alone terrifies him in a very primal way. He wants to be part of the group—to fit in and be accepted, not to be seen as a renegade, or worse, a dissident.

What this executive can't see is that others would accept him and respect him all the more if they could only see him stand up for what's important to him. They may not agree with his viewpoint, but they will respect him for having the courage to speak up and make himself heard.

Since the executive has little experience in this area, he's likely to jump to the conclusion that you're suggesting he start an open rebellion or junta against the prevailing direction of the organization. Of course, this isn't what you're suggesting, but his fear tells him that all expressions of individuation are extreme. You've got to carefully show him there is a more moderate path.

Courage to do great things always begins in small ways. To begin, help the executive focus on small ways he can express his opinion to powerful others. Start with an issue or project that isn't critical. Encourage him to tell the CEO that he doesn't believe the plan will work, or that he has a great idea for an improvement on an existing product. It shouldn't be anything earth-shattering or potentially disastrous to his career. On the other hand, it should be something that stretches him just a little further than he's been willing to stretch before. Let's return to the case of Carolyn for an example:

CASE STUDY

COURAGE COMES THROUGH ACTION

As a training manager, Carolyn had suffered for years from a crisis individuation and paralysis analysis. Her first step toward discovering courage was to tell her boss, the senior vice president of human resources, that the customer-service training program wasn't working. The program had been the brainchild of her boss, who had sold the idea at the top of the organization as a way to improve customer retention. Unfortunately, the firm he had suggested Carolyn hire to conduct the program just wasn't interested in tailoring the training program to the organization's specific needs. They were insisting on teaching a generic program that, among other things, used case studies that were completely foreign to the employees. The standard complaint of employees who took the program was that the training seemed targeted more toward a manufacturing company than a service company, like theirs.

Carolyn knew that her boss had worked with this training company before and was good friends with its president. She knew that the last thing her boss wanted to hear was that the training wasn't working as well as he had told the senior executives it would.

With some coaching, Carolyn decided to meet with her boss and take a sample of the training evaluations. Her objective for the meeting was to simply plant the idea that the training might not be as effective as it could be. She wasn't going to harshly criticize the training firm or paint too dire a picture for her boss. She was just going to plant a seed.

After the meeting, Carolyn was quite surprised by her boss's reaction. He immediately understood what she was suggesting about the training and even mentioned that he had seen the same problem with that firm before. He thanked Carolyn for letting him know about the problems and gave her full authority to ask the firm to redesign the training program or even fire them if necessary.

To someone who isn't in a crisis of individuation, Carolyn's meeting with her boss might not seem all that important, but it was wildly important to Carolyn. Before this meeting she would have put a positive spin on the training and tried to do as much damage control as possible so that her boss wouldn't look bad. She would have spent enormous time and effort trying to contain the problem rather than go against her boss's recommendation.

Now, Carolyn has discovered the courage to speak out on those issues that are important to her and her job, even when it means contradicting someone in power. She hasn't always prevailed, but she's definitely earned the respect of her peers and her superiors as someone who is a solid leader.

Courage doesn't happen overnight. It doesn't come with insight. You can't give it to someone. Courage comes only one way: through action.

To help your client find the courage he needs to resolve the crisis, you've got to help him get moving. Only when he sees himself doing what he thought he could never do will he feel the courage within himself to keep doing it. Courage is the result of a self-perpetuating cycle that once started, builds upon itself. The coach starts this cycle by insisting on small, positive steps. Courage then follows naturally.

It's not easy for any of us to become an individual. There are so many temptations to abandon ourselves, our values, and our passions along the way. It takes a great deal of courage to stand up for your convictions, for there's always a chance that those convictions may prove to be wrong. It takes courage to stare down the rants of self-doubt and the fear of abandonment.

As a coach, you must always look inside yourself and your own experience to truly understand and help your client. To help a client suffering from a crisis of individuation, you must first understand your own struggle to individuate. When you do, you can gently guide your client to discover the courage we all have within ourselves, no matter how deeply it's buried, to become a strong and passionate individual.

Confronting the Parent/Child Messages

A big part of resolving a crisis of individuation lies in sorting out or "decontaminating" the executive's ego states. The old Child and Parent messages are familiar and automatic, encouraging the client to engage in the same behaviors that he's always acted out. Those behaviors don't work and by now he probably sees that, but the old patterns are doggedly persistent and lead him to the same frustrating point every time.

The coach must spot these intrusions of Parent and Child messages and help the client to examine their content. For example, when the client remarks that "I'm nice guy . . . I want everyone to like me," the coach might begin to help the client sort out the ego origins of that message. Is he choosing to be a "nice guy," or is he being driven to do so by an old parental mandate?

The client who suffers from a crisis of individuation often experiences a number of negative and automatic messages. Here are a few of the Parent/Child messages that I've seen clients in a crisis of individuation struggle with.

MY VALUE AS A PERSON COMES FROM THE ORGANIZATION/COMPANY I BELONG TO

A surprising number of executives derive a great deal of ego strength from their association with an important organization. These executives *need* to belong to a company that they believe makes them appear better than they believe themselves to be. Whenever something happens that makes them feel as if they aren't squarely in the center of the organization's power conduit, they panic. "If I'm not working for IBM, then I'm nothing," they seem to tell themselves. Over and over again they repeat this thought, convincing themselves their personal value is at stake.

This automatic statement causes the executive to do whatever he thinks will put him back in the good graces of the organization's power structure. Now, at first glance this kind of thinking might seem to be appropriate for creating a focused organization, but the net effect is actually quite damaging to the organization. The executive's attention is slowly siphoned off by his need to please others rather than to manage the work effectively.

Coaching can help this executive to revise his automatic statements and instead say, "I am an expert at what I do, no matter where I work" and "My value as a person is far more than what I do or for whom I work." Teaching the client to repeat these statements whenever he begins to fear rejection from his employer can be a powerful tool in building the courage to change.

CONFLICT WITH OTHERS SHOULD BE AVOIDED AT ALL COSTS

To be human is to experience conflict, for certain. There is no way to live and work with other people without experiencing conflict. When an executive tries to avoid conflict, he inevitably creates a more difficult situation down the road.

CASE
STUDY

CONFLICT CAN BE GOOD

Joan was the manager of a sales division for an industrial supply company who avoided conflict with her employees at all
costs. Joan's division covered four states in the Southwest
that contained several large metropolitan areas and also large
sparsely populated areas. Some of the salespeople who
reported to her covered large rural territories; others had relatively small areas of high-density population. Those who
worked the rural territories had grown increasingly frustrated with the large amount of travel and time required to
make even the smallest of sales, especially compared to the
territories in urban areas. The urban sales orders were often
large and a single trip to one city could easily accommodate
visits to many customers.

The conflict between the rural and urban salespeople had
grown increasingly hot, especially since the urban salespeople often made twice as much in commissions.Realizing that
no matter what she did someone would be unhappy with
her, Joan did nothing. She would put off the rural salespeople by telling them she was studying the situation and that
she'd do what was best for the company. She was unwilling
to make the urban salespeople angry by redistributing some
of their clients to the rural salespeople, so her only choice
was to try to maintain the situation as best as possible.

The consequence of Joan's inaction was to create turmoil
among the salespeople and fuel growing frustration among
the disgruntled rural sales force. Many of her best rural salespeople left for better jobs as sales in their territories steadily
declined. The numbers for Joan's division began to show a
serious decline and rumors about the unhappy sales force
began to spread throughout the company. Her boss began to
question her ability to run the division and gave her six
months to fix the problem if she wanted to keep her job.

Coaching helped Joan to change her automatic statements about conflict. Instead of reflexively telling herself that conflict must be avoided, she learned to tell herself that conflict can be healthy and lead to better solutions, if handled properly. Eventually, Joan was able to call a three-day meeting with all of her employees to discuss the problem and various solutions. Ultimately, what the group decided was to redistribute some of the more lucrative accounts, giving them to the more difficult rural territories. Not everyone was overjoyed with the solution, but it was something everyone felt they could live with, and consequently, it resolved the conflict.

I CAN BE SUCCESSFUL ONLY IF EVERYONE LIKES ME

Some executives use their popularity in the organization as barometer of their success. If most everyone likes them, then they feel they are doing a good job. Take the case of Eric:

> Eric is a human resources manager for an international retailer that recently was forced to downsize. Eric's job became central to the downsizing—helping managers select who would be laid off, when they would be fired, and how much severance pay would be given. Very quickly Eric discovered that nobody likes to go through a downsizing, and no matter what he did, he couldn't please everyone. The managers were angry that he was forcing them to lay off employees and the employees were angry about possibly being laid off. No matter what decisions he made, his job was despised by almost everyone. The stress and anxiety was so great, Eric began suffering from panic attacks and was forced to take a leave of absence from work.

Coaching this executive requires teaching him that success has little to do with popularity. Most of the world's greatest executives are quite unpopular with some of their employees and

141

associates. It's just the nature of being an executive—someone isn't going to like how you do your job. For an executive to hold himself to the impossible standard of trying to please everyone is to create a personal disaster. He'll never meet that goal and he'll find himself constantly frustrated trying to reach it.

Success is best defined by the realization of one's passion in life; it's not about how much other people like you. Doing a great job at what you love to do is the Holy Grail that brings lasting satisfaction and fulfillment to the executive. In the process of realizing his passion, he will make friends who will support his work. Others—and there are always the detractors—will be displeased and perhaps even oppose him.

Some business situations require an executive to make a highly unpopular decision for the sake of the business. Ultimately, that decision may win the respect of others, but at the time it is made, some aren't happy with the outcome. Decisions to discontinue an old product line or to close a facility can be lonely decisions to make. The executive who gauges his success by his work and not his popularity may not enjoy such tasks, but he's free to make those unpopular decisions. At the end of the day, the executive who knows the difference is the one who earns the respect that leadership demands.

T E N

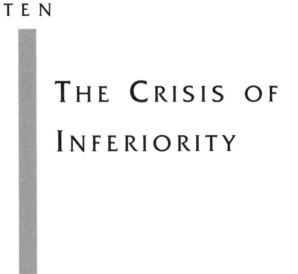

THE CRISIS OF INFERIORITY

Say what you will, but I never let anyone get the upper hand with me. I know it's not fashionable to say it these days, but business is about winning, not making friends. When I hire new employees, I tell them, "Look, this is my department and you will do things my way. As long as I look good, you've got a job."

Winning is all about strategy, and I'm a great strategist. Sometimes I wake up in the middle of the night
thinking about how I'll handle such-and-such a situation. I don't trust anyone, least of all other department heads. Turn your head for a minute, and they'll
rob you blind every time. More than once I've lost
the credit for a successful project because another
department head claimed credit for it. I'm telling
you, it's every man for himself, and if you don't
believe that, you're fooling yourself.

I make a point of making my accomplishments
known to senior management because that's the
only way they'll ever know what I can do. A little personal PR never did anyone harm. You've got to let
them know just whom they're dealing with . . . .

"Everyone else must lose in order for me to win." "I take
what is my due before someone else does." "Business is always
every-man-for-himself." These are the thoughts behind the
actions of the executive suffering from a crisis of inferiority. He
believes that ultimately he must belittle or destroy others—and
that includes colleagues, bosses, and employees—if they become
a barrier to what he wants. This executive is perpetually aware of
the power of those around him and how they might use that
power to diminish his success. Business is a survival game for
him where he must ultimately prove himself better than everyone else with whom he works.
    So what does he do? He must try to make those who
threaten him powerless and hence diminish his own sense of
powerlessness. The tragic truth is that this executive believes
himself to be inferior to those around him and is constantly
about the task of proving to himself and everyone else that he
isn't inferior. It never works—he's always left feeling inferior
regardless of the conquest—so he must move on to greater challenges.
    The crisis is triggered and becomes inflamed usually
when the executive has lost most of his support in the organization as a result of his backhanded deals and self-promotion. He

befriends those who can help him, but only uses them to get what he wants. Over time, other executives recognize this trick and begin to withdraw, unless he becomes so powerful that they feel they must accommodate him to preserve their own careers. Either way, he builds a large, silent audience that is quietly hoping for his demise.

When something big falls apart for him, no one is there to help. His fall from power can be precipitous and shockingly quick. That's usually when you encounter this executive in crisis.

Everyone Else Is More Successful Than I Am

The executive with a crisis of inferiority is his own worst critic. He holds himself to a very tough standard—one that he will never achieve. He is relentlessly driving himself to succeed. When others succeed, he is quietly jealous and condemns himself because he's not the one in the spotlight. He notices that others don't have to work as hard as he does at success; then he uses this information to convince himself that he's inferior to them. This, of course, only drives him to work harder, be more manipulative, and be heavy-handed in his job.

When his crisis explodes in full fury, he may become despondent—and a few have even become suicidal. (Should you encounter a suicidal executive, immediately refer him to an appropriate mental health professional. A coach is not equipped to work with such serious and life-threatening feelings.) The world seems to cave in on him and swallow him up. He's worked hard, damn hard, and what has he gotten? Failure.

Because he is so hard on himself, this executive rewrites all his successes into failures when in crisis. He thinks he hasn't done anything very well and has missed far too many opportunities. If only he had worked harder. If only he had gotten the promotion. If only he had seized the opportunity. If only.

He may be so distraught that he is unable to work; possibly he's been fired because he couldn't function on the job anymore. He may feel anger at others, but when you get to the bottom of his feelings, he's mostly angry with himself.

Better to Bully Than to Be Bullied

An executive who has an unresolved crisis of inferiority has a management style best described as bullying. He uses a heavy hand in wielding power to get what he wants, and the more he thinks he can get away with it, the more he bullies.

C A S E
S T U D Y

BIG MAN ON CAMPUS

Dan worked for an advertising firm. A former professional football player, he was full of energy and great with clients, exuding a self-confidence that inspired their faith in the firm. Dan's tough-guy attitude seemed to match the macho image of the firm and its founding president. He rose quickly through the ranks, but throughout his career his big-man-on-campus attitude never changed. His favorites, known to the disgruntled in the firm as Dan's Do-Gooders, moved forward with him. Like a clique of top jocks, they went around oblivious to, or disdainful of, the talented but less egotistical staff on whom the success of the firm depended.

Dan's appointment as president signaled to the staff that his aggressive management style was the way of the future. His superior attitude fostered jealousy and divisiveness. Everyone kept busy—some trying to impress Dan so they could snag favored assignments, others moaning about their lack of status in the firm; quite a few employees began to hastily write their resumes. Projects failed. Deadlines were missed. The firm became less and less likely to fulfill Dan's promises to the clients. It lost several important accounts.

Blindsided by a lifetime of success as a charging bull, Dan decided to take an action guaranteed to exacerbate the problem. At a meeting called to discuss strategies for dealing with falling revenues, he announced his management approach—

the credo of bullies everywhere. "It's time," he said, "to kick ass and take names."

Dan's actions aggravated the morale problems and led to even higher turnover and further loss of business. Yet his actions were based on what had worked for him in the past: coercion and punishment. This time, though, it only hastened the impending disaster.

What's important to notice about this kind of executive is that at first sight he appears confident and powerful. He may deal with his employees as if he never had a self-doubt. Often the executive isn't the stereotypic image of what you might think inferiority looks like.

But the stereotypic image is wrong. Executives suffering from inferiority make up for their self-doubts by presenting an image of power and control. It's far too threatening for them to allow anyone to see their vulnerable side, so they cover it up with a façade of imperiousness. They fear you will discover their inferiority and then destroy them. If you threaten to come too close to that vulnerable, self-doubting side of them, they will try to destroy you first—or, at least, domineer you and render you powerless.

Make no mistake about it; a bully can make his way all the way from the mailroom to the executive suite without his crisis of inferiority becoming inflamed. In fact, not a few executives have built entire careers using their instinctive and well-practiced bullying techniques.

As a coach, however, you're only concerned with those executives who are experiencing their crisis of inferiority, and that's when the bully has hit very hard times. He has walked a tight rope of arrogance, manipulation, and power plays for a long time, and when he falls, there is no net to save him.

A Corporate Grifter

Another circumstance that an executive with a crisis inferiority might create is a career that has promised much and delivered little, yet always moves forward. These executives often surround themselves with the trappings of expertise. They might get higher degrees, industry-specific credentials, and training certificates. Their job title and position in the organization is very important to them, and they remind others of their credentials as often as they can.

C A S E
S T U D Y
A HOLLOW CAREER

According to his resume, Eric was an expert in quality assurance training. He claimed to have designed and implemented several large-scale quality programs in Fortune 500 companies. It appeared he had been very successful, for each job had moved him up a level or two, and he was now the director of quality assurance for a very prominent media empire.

The problem was that Eric had never delivered on his promises. Starting in his first position as a quality engineer, Eric had discovered a quality-training consulting firm that had developed a comprehensive system of training and quality assurance programs. Eric hired them in his first job and had used the consulting firm in every job since then.

Every two years, Eric jumped from company to company. He stayed in a job just long enough to sell the idea of implementing a comprehensive quality-training curriculum and process, hire the consulting firm, and implement the first training programs. He was then off to the next job. Eric never stayed anywhere long enough to really know, or prove, that the programs he implemented really improved quality. In fact, there were some disgruntled ex-bosses who would suggest that the programs were a waste of money.

Eric knew the lingo of the quality world. He knew the issues and catch phrases, and they rolled off his tongue with the greatest of ease. If you spent any time with Eric, you'd probably walk away convinced he knew something about quality improvement.

Eric knew the training materials backward and forward. He knew what the current quality fads were. Ironically, Eric had never actually done the work of quality improvement.

Eric covered his crisis of inferiority by learning the talk of his field. As long as he kept moving from job to job, no one discovered his incompetence before he was gone. He would always spin the achievements in his previous job into something more than they really were, get the next job, and move to another level in a new organization. That's how he climbed to the top.

Now that Eric was in a top quality position at an international firm, he was overwhelmed. This firm had already gone down the quality-training road and hadn't seen much gain for the money. They hired Eric to do something different, and hopefully, better.

The pressure on Eric steadily increased to produce something of value. All the while, though, Eric shopped for consultants to save him. He brought in a steady stream of programs and consultants, but senior management wasn't impressed with the window dressing. They wanted results, and they wanted them *yesterday*. Eric was in fine mess.

Executives may try to handle their crisis of inferiority by "hovering above the work." That is, they never really do the work for which they are responsible. Like our case study executive Eric, they learn to talk the talk and appear as experts, but they are experts without any experience. If they were to stay long enough to engage in the work, someone might discover their inferiority and that would be disastrous. Better to appear to be the expert than to do the work and risk making mistakes. The higher they rise in the organization, the riskier it becomes to reveal that they don't really know what they're doing.

The Fear Complex

An executive with a deeply held fear complex of feeling inferior to others may think he is somehow lacking something essential he needs—something everyone else appears to have. To protect himself and his career, he must conquer everyone else to protect his essential vulnerability. As long as he has everyone else scared, they won't discover his imagined inferiority.

This fear complex of inferiority has probably been with him for most of his life. In school he feared that he wouldn't make the grade or the varsity team. He probably chooses friends who aren't threatening to him. Just as soon as a friend becomes more successful than he has been, he's likely to drop the friendship. At work, this executive's fear complex of inferiority can manifest itself in many ways, including hiring employees he knows have little potential of outshining him. He likes to be king of his department and doesn't handle criticism or superstar employees very well. In his mind, his survival hinges upon his ability to overpower his challengers before they discover his critical vulnerability.

Understanding the Life Script

The insight that holds great promise for the client with a crisis of inferiority is this: He has lived most of his life as if he were in competition with everyone around him—and he always feels as if he's come in second place.

That insight into his life script is profound and can potentially shake the foundations of his life. Somewhere in his lifetime he was forced to meet expectations that he could never achieve. A parent pushed him as a child to be something extraordinary, and no matter how hard he tried, he never was good enough. Or a coach demanded more of him than he could give and shamed him when he failed to achieve. Or he was placed in a demanding job too early in his career and he failed because of lack of experience, but never let himself off the hook for having failed.

Whatever the significant event, it utterly convinced him that he was inferior to others. He has a lifelong history of eliminating his competition before it eliminates him, for he is certain that's what the competition will do if given the chance—destroy him.

This executive is always about the business of trying to convince that nagging Parent voice inside him that he isn't inferior. To do this, he attempts ever-greater challenges and feats that will prove him superior, but no matter how great the success, he never accepts it as evidence that he isn't inferior. He might quietly think that he got lucky or was in the right place at the right time. Rarely, if ever, does he truly allow himself to accept his own accomplishments as evidence of his true skill.

The insight this executive needs is to realize that he has been pushed by his sense of inferiority rather than guided by his passion for most of his life. Rather than following his own interests and desires, he may have chosen a course of study in college that he thought was extraordinarily challenging or would lead him into a super-successful career. His job choices were most likely based solely on pay and prestige rather than the job he would most enjoy.

Realizing that you've spent most of your life running from your own internal demon can be both deeply troubling and wildly liberating. Learning how to let go of the struggle for superiority, savor your successes, and follow your passion is what this insight can lead to. As a coach, your responsibility isn't to protect the client from the pain of his script, but to channel that pain into a path that will lead him out of a script and into free choice. You encourage him to feel the pain of having spent his life trying to be "better than" and at the same time offer suggestions of alternative paths that are dictated by his suppressed passion.

The kinds of coaching questions that are useful with this client include:

"If you could do anything where money and success weren't an issue, what would you do?"

"Aren't you tired of fighting the playground bullies?"

"How far will you have to go to finally feel successful?"

"When will you start really living and enjoying your life?"

Once the client sees the lifelong pattern of struggling for superiority, you're ready to begin the process of helping him break the pattern.

Finding the Courage

This executive needs to discover the courage to participate in a group or a relationship where he doesn't dominate. At first glance, you may wonder if courage is what is really needed. (Maybe what he really needs is a good dose of humility?) From his perspective, participation without domination takes a great deal of courage, and if you want to help him, you've got to understand this.

As we have seen, there are many examples of an executive who spends all his life as if he were in a competition—for love, success, money, friendship, you name it—with everyone in his life. To deny this fear and be part of a team where he isn't driving the action takes courage on his part. He will have to fight a good battle against feelings of failure and inferiority in such a situation. Let's look at an example to clarify what this feels like to the client.

C A S E
S T U D Y

THE COURAGE TO PARTICIPATE, NOT DOMINATE

Mark is the sales director for a large, multinational life insurance company. He worked his way up from door-to-door sales and cold calling to become one of the company's most successful sales representatives in its seventy-five-year history. Now that Mark holds a corporate position that is far removed from the actual selling of life insurance, he feels the need to establish his credentials as one of the company's all-time leading salespersons by trying to outdo every new person with whom he works.

Whenever Mark is in a meeting, he tries to dominate the discussion with his opinion of what would be best for company sales. He demonstrates little tolerance for others' opinions, especially if he senses that the person didn't come up through the ranks of life insurance sales. Toward staff departments such as human resources or operations, he shows little respect and gives those departments only the required minimal amount of his time and attention.

Behind Mark's back, others joke about his "war stories" on the sales beat. He's told some of the same stories hundreds of times (the ones that always show him as the expert salesman). Employees would say to each other things like: "Did he tell you the one about . . . ?" or "I can't believe he told that one again!"

Mark's tendency to credential himself and dominate meetings had created a great deal of trouble for him—trouble that after twenty years he was just now beginning to understand. Other people avoided including him in meetings and would work around him if at all possible. Sure, everyone respected him as a great former salesman, but very few wanted to work directly with him.

Coaching Mark meant starting with small steps toward the courage to participate while not dominating. One of the first steps he took was to hold an off-site meeting with his staff to plan for the next year. In very uncharacteristic style, he allowed one of his staff members to set the agenda and run the meeting. Everyone was apprehensive and skeptical about what was happening, expecting the old Mark to jump in and take over. The off-site meeting lagged and for a day and a half didn't seem to go anywhere. Mark was uncomfortable with the pace and was simply itching to assert his authority and get things moving. Luckily (and with some constant coaching on the side) he refrained.

On the second half of the second day, his staff began to emerge in a way they hadn't done before. They brought up important issues that they had previously been unwilling to voice and began to work together to suggest improvements to the department. By the end of that day, the meeting had made great strides toward creating the plan for the next year.

Mark was impressed by the results, and as the year progressed, people in the company were taking notice, so he was even more impressed by how nicely those results reflected on him. Slowly, he learned that he didn't have to always be the aggressor to win. He could allow others to assert themselves and it could work to everyone's advantage, even his own.

It takes small steps of courage for many executives to learn to let go of their authority whip and allow others to shine. The more steps taken, however, the more courageous you become. The courage to not dominate when you feel that your career well-being is always at stake is won slowly. The executive who suffers from a crisis of inferiority becomes less dominating in small steps. Only once he gains the confidence to allow others to flourish will he help his career, not harm it. And, he will discover the courage he needs to completely resolve this crisis.

Confronting the Parent/Child Messages

There are certain automatic Parent/Child messages that reinforce a crisis of inferiority. Let's review some of them and see which ones you'll recognize.

When Others Near Me Succeed, It Makes Me Feel Like a Failure

This executive tells himself that when others succeed it proves his inferiority. As a result, other people's successes threaten him. He may make a big show of congratulatory gestures to cover up his feelings of inferiority, but underneath he feels threatened.

This automatic statement becomes even more absurd when the executive's own successes are considered objectively. Often the executive has achieved much success on his own. Clearly, his own success has little to do with his feelings about the successes of others.

CASE STUDY

THE SILENT SABOTEUR

John was the youngest of four children and always felt he was in competition with his two older brothers. They were both very smart, and star athletes to boot, so all his young life he was compared to them. His teachers always expected him to be at least as good a student as his brothers had been.

By all accounts, John was also bright and talented. Nevertheless, he carried with him a sense of inferiority. During his mid-thirties, John was promoted to vice president of strategic planning for a large software company. His job was one of the most exciting and nerve-racking in the company—looking into the crystal ball to see what new technologies were lurking just around the corner that would affect the company's products. One day the programming language X is hot, the next day, it is obsolete. It was John's job to anticipate and prepare the company for the industry changes that were coming down the pike.

John had achieved remarkable success in his position. He was one of the youngest vice presidents in the company and, by far, one of the highest-paid executives. The CEO trusted John's judgment completely and repeatedly let him know how valuable he was to the company.

Despite all this, John was threatened by a smart, young manager who reported to him. The young manager had moved up through the ranks quickly, just as John had done. The more and the harder the manager worked, the more difficult John made his job. Without seeming aggressive toward the manager, John made his life very difficult. Eventually, he even transferred the manager to the Austin, Texas facility, far away from the company's headquarters in Silicon Valley. Not surprisingly, the manager eventually left the company to take another position with a competitor.

What John did to the young manager really isn't all that

uncommon. Because he had taught himself that other people's success might diminish his own, he made a point of quietly undermining the success of those who threatened him. He never did anything overtly destructive, but when the opportunity came to silently sabotage their success, he would usually act on it.

OTHERS ARE ALWAYS DOUBTING MY CAPABILITY, SO I MUST CONSTANTLY PROVE MYSELF TO THEM

The executive who tells himself that others are always ready to doubt his competence is forced to always prove them wrong. It is a tiring and stressful task that is never fully completed. This is the Child performing at top speed, hoping to win the approval of others.

Unfortunately, this executive's constant "bravado" becomes annoying, to say the least, and his relationships falter. Other people tire of his need to prove himself and win accolades. The problem that begins to kill his success isn't his lack of competence but his obnoxious need to prove himself.

During one of my consulting assignments with a team of executives who reported to a senior vice president named Tom, one of the executives came up to me and asked me privately: "Did Tom tell you the Portland story? The distribution reorganization story? *The Wall Street Journal* story?"

The fact was, Tom had told me these stories . . . and within the first hour of meeting him. Each of these stories conveyed to Tom's listeners the extent of his biggest successes, and he repeated them over and over until everyone knew them by heart. I don't think that Tom knew how tired and bored everyone was with them.

Tom told himself that everyone suspected his incompetence, so he needed to prove them wrong. Since they might not have seen him in action, he repeated his "greatest hits" so they wouldn't forget. And they didn't. To Tom, those stories were proof of his success; to everyone else they had become jokes with Tom as the punch line.

Coaching executives like Tom requires that you provide them with another paradigm. Other people usually assume that he is competent, until circumstances prove otherwise. The real doubter isn't the audience here, it's the actor. Tom was mostly trying to prove to himself that he was competent. Every time he repeated those stories he could glean a bit of pride over what he had done and, for the moment, assuage the nagging doubts in his own mind.

I Should Never Admit Failure

Sometimes the greatest remedy to failure is simply to own it. When someone, even a top executive, says "I made a mistake," it's much easier to move on and fix the problem. When executives refuse to acknowledge (much less admit) a mistake, the problem often grows worse and feelings become bitter.

There can be great power in owning an injury, both personally and professionally. Rachel Hubka, the president of the $3.5 million Rachel's Bus Company, tells the story of admitting a mistake and what it did for her business. It provides a good case study for any executive.

CASE STUDY

OWNING UP

Rachel built her company on the fact that she had spotless buses, sent computerized confirmations of all orders, and had well-trained drivers who wore suits and ties.

After one of her drivers failed to get a charter of eighth-graders to their destination on time, Rachel had the choice of either blaming a few late-arriving children for the delay or owning the mistake and refunding the $3,200 fee. It would have been very easy, according to Rachel, to simply fault the children and keep the deposit, except for one problem—the driver privately admitted that he hadn't studied the map and had got lost on the way. When the school called and complained to Rachel, she admitted the mistake and refunded the fee. The result? The school remained a loyal customer.

Often the admission of a mistake strengthens a relationship. Coaching the executive who uses this automatic statement requires helping him to see that being vulnerable and human rather than blameless and perfect strengthens his business relationships. People want to work for and do business with someone they trust—someone who isn't afraid to admit it when they falter.

ELEVEN

THE CRISIS

OF ISOLATION

I'm tired. I have to admit it. You get tired of the intense stupidity around here. It's been a long time. Oh, there've been some good things—I won't say there haven't been some bright guys among the general clunks—but the fact is, I should have gotten out long ago. Now it's too late—there are the mortgage payments and alimony and support and I have to say it's comfortable here and where else can I get that income?

Have you ever read our recruiting brochures or listened to the speeches by our president? "We are meeting the challenges," they say, or brilliant insights like, "The future lies before us . . . " My God . . . and here we are in middle management, a bunch of middle-age drudges, a lot of losers . . . .

Well, all you have to do around here is step on the creeping escalator and keep your nose clean and you go on up with the rest of the drudges and morons. On the way, I've seen guys who could barely tie their shoelaces reach positions where they could sit on their fat asses and make life miserable for everybody else. It just happened—they promoted an idiot and now he's got more people to make miserable.

What I object to most is the waste of people around here—myself included. I've been passed over twice now, so I guess you can say I'm bitter about that, and it's true I am. But I look back at even the good times and I think mine has been a career wasted in a clueless organization. So few of my talents are used, and even when they are, there's usually some corporate jerk who manages to screw up the good I've done.

I've been blessed with a fairly high IQ and stupidity does something to me that I can't quite explain, so lately my frustration has gone through the roof. Lots of executives can put up with it, but not me. Last year a competitor developed a piece of equipment somewhat similar to the one we were developing, though ours would have been much more sophisticated. Then, a recession hit our major markets. For the first time our profits took a bad tumble and the storm warnings were everywhere. If we'd had management with just a little vision, if we'd even had

> management with some guts, our project would
> have survived and weathered the storm. But
> instead, we have a company run by idiots . . . .

John was totally disgusted by the memo from corporate. Lately, he was disgusted by everything coming from corporate. As far as John was concerned, those suits didn't have a clue as to how the real world worked. He threw the memo in the circular file where all the others had gone before. If those know-it-alls needed something from him, they'd just have to come down here and ask for it themselves.

Sue had worked for the bank for twenty-five years. Although the bank had far outgrown its local roots to become the biggest bank in Washington state and one of the largest nation-wide, Sue ran her human resource department like she did in the good old days when she could easily visit every branch office in one day. Now, with more than 1,000 branches across the country, she hadn't set foot in more than half the branches. But none of this really mattered. Sue was the company expert in labor relations and government regulations regarding bank employees. She handled all grievances personally. Her department made sure that everyone was paid on time and all the benefit programs ran smoothly. That's what human resources (it was called personnel back when she was first put in charge) was all about, and she knew the routine like clockwork. She regularly turned down requests from company managers for flexible work time, job sharing, modified benefit plans, and sabbatical leaves. These weren't standard programs. Her philosophy was to "stick to the knitting" and everything will turn out fine.

Greg was the director of design for a retail products firm. Over the years, he had a few smash successes with redesigned products and consequently was promoted to the top design position. Greg felt he knew everything about product design and he created a design process that he expected every designer in his department to follow, regardless of the requests from the marketing department or elsewhere in the company. He believed no one else in the company was qualified to make design decisions and as a result, had little use for their input. Eventually, during a corporate headquarters remodel, Greg was able to move his department to a separate building across town from the main office. There, Greg felt he would be better able to help his department focus solely on good design without all the corporate runaround.

What do John, Sue, and Greg have in common? A crisis of isolation. The crisis of isolation may appear in many different forms, but it always has the distinct component of wall building to separate the executive and his department from the rest of the organization. Whether those walls are physical (as in the case of Greg), in policy (as in the case of Sue), or in reduced communication (as in the case of John), they are intended to isolate the executive.

Why would any executive want to isolate himself? The answer is simple: *power.* Without interference from other parts of the organization, the executive can build an empire that he runs almost exclusively.

The power that the executive with a crisis of isolation is seeking is power to protect himself from others. In almost all cases, the crisis of isolation is triggered by a perceived betrayal. The betrayal may have come in the form of being denied a promised promotion, having a colleague steal credit for accomplishments, or being double-crossed by another executive.

The betrayal triggers the crisis that comes from some very deep feelings of disappointment and hurt by other people. The result is that this executive withdraws and attempts to protect himself by drawing a distinct line of territory and ruling that territory singularly.

I'm Disappointed in People

The crisis of isolation feels like a general disappointment and frustration with other people in the organization. This executive has little patience for the shortcomings of other executives and generally overinterprets any actions that appear negative toward him. He has given up on trying to effectively work with others, except where he knows he must in order to retain his position. "What's the point of waiting around for another person to do something halfway, when I can do it right in less time?"

C A S E
S T U D Y

WHAT'S THE POINT OF ALL THAT WORK?

Joan was the "queen of claims processing" (her real job title). She worked for an insurance company that had been in business for more than one hundred years and had a reputation for being somewhat staid and bureaucratic. In an effort to loosen up things in modern times, the company had initiated many programs, including coming up with some hip-sounding job titles.

Several years ago, Joan had been part of an executive committee that was charged with reorganizing the operations side of the organization. It was a huge task and involved enormous research, consultations, and input from employees all over the company. In the end, the committee had completed its assignment with a detailed reorganization plan that they were convinced was the best possible configuration for their insurance business in the current economic environment.

Unfortunately, Joan's boss, a senior executive vice president, didn't care much for the committee's recommendations and pushed Joan to make changes to them. Joan, not agreeing with her boss, made a half-hearted attempt to suggest the changes, and of course, nothing changed.

Joan's boss stood to lose some of his organization, and consequently his status, if the recommended reorganization was implemented. He began to work against the committee behind the scenes, eventually convincing the CEO that an outside consulting firm should be hired to design the reorganization. So, after several years of hard work, the committee's recommendations were completely discarded.

What was the point of all that work? It seemed clear to Joan that nothing mattered but an executive's power, if he was willing to completely disregard such a well-designed reorganization plan. How much money and time had the organ-

163

ization wasted on that committee? It made her shudder to think about it.

The worst part was having to face all those managers and employees who had volunteered their time and energy to provide the committee with data. They had been promised results that never came, as a result of the disregarded reorganization plan. Most of them didn't understand the political dynamic that had prevented the plan's implementation, and given the dynamic between Joan and her boss, she wasn't free to share the truth. Consequently, Joan felt that she came out of the whole affair looking foolish, if not somewhat incompetent.

That experience burned her badly. Slowly she began to withdraw from all but the most essential corporate projects, preferring to keep her head low and manage her claims processing division. Other executives began to complain that she and her department were not responsive to their queries and weren't willing to be flexible as change was needed.

Joan's language was filled with blame for other departments and executives, but especially for her boss. She was careful to document everything she did and lived "strictly by the book." She was proud that her claims department had achieved what she called "excellence," and completely ignored the complaints as superfluous and political in nature. She said she didn't "play politics" and couldn't understand why senior management allowed so much political maneuvering to happen.

With a little probing, Joan's bitterness over the failed reorganization plan spilled from her. She felt the whole affair had been a waste of her time, and she was determined to never again involve herself in such a project. Instead, she would work only on those projects she could control. That way, no one with personal or political aspirations could hurt her the way that the reorganization fiasco had.

Retreat and Entrench

One way of handling the crisis of isolation is for the executive to entrench himself in standard policies and procedures. The policy manual—for whatever the task or function—can become a great shield to hide behind. An executive who hides behind the policy manual often will make statements such as: "No, I can't do that . . . it's not standard procedure," or "That's not the way we do things in this department," or "It might be a good idea, but it's against policy."

This executive becomes rigid and inflexible, using standard procedures and policies as his excuse for being unwilling to change. Those policies protect him from the harm he imagines others will do to his career. He can't be blamed—and in his mind he should be given a medal—for upholding company policy.

Obviously, company policy must be established and respected. Nonetheless, everyone knows that policy is an ongoing evolution and as business changes, the policies must change, too. New problems sometimes require new policies.

The executive with a crisis of isolation refuses to evolve policy because that would require becoming vulnerable to others. Policy is never changed in a vacuum, and it requires the input of others in the organization. Plus, there is a certain risk in making any change.

All of this makes changing policy very difficult for the executive with a crisis of isolation. He doesn't want to risk the vulnerability involved, so he sticks to the status quo. It's safer for him that way.

If I Want It Done Right, I'd Better Do It Myself

"Nobody does it quite the way I want it done." "It will take more time to explain what I want than it will for me to do it myself." "I can't trust this job to anyone else." To put it bluntly, the executive who talks like that has a serious problem with delegation. Oh, he may give a job to someone else to do, but he does so only after he tells him exactly how to do the job. He can't trust that others might have a better way of working than he does, because he doesn't trust that they will do it right.

CASE
STUDY

THE MICROMANAGER

Peter is an executive director of a nonprofit organization that has a staff of ten employees. Although he was educated at Harvard, he worked his way up the organization ladder from secretary all the way to executive director. In between, Peter had held every position in the organization.

Before being named executive director, Peter thought the former executive director had betrayed him when she sent a letter to the board of trustees recommending that Peter not be given the top job,. He was crushed and deeply hurt by her actions. But all of that was a long time ago, and after Peter had served as "acting executive director" for several years, the board finally gave him the permanent title.

Peter was convinced that no one in organization had as much as experience as he did, despite the fact that several had far more years of nonprofit work experience than he did. He insisted that everyone in the organization do their job just as he had done it when he was in each position. Subtly but regularly, he would remind the staff that no one had written and received more grants than when he was development director, or that he had in one year handled more grant requests when he was program director than any other program director.

Peter's crisis of isolation prevented him from trusting the wisdom and skills of his employees. Instead, he was compelled to micromanage every job and project in the organization, which caused him to work endless hours more than were necessary. He proofread every document and letter, always finding something to change. He involved himself in every fund-raising activity, no matter how small, and every grant-making activity, no matter how experienced the employee who was handling it.

As a result, Peter couldn't keep employees. They would usually stay a year or two, and when they realized that Peter would never trust them to do their jobs, they would move on to other organizations. This, of course, only confirmed Peter's belief that "you can't hire good help" and "if you want a job done right, you better do it yourself."

The Fear Complex

The core of the crisis of isolation is a painful fear complex of betrayal. Somewhere along the way, the person has felt betrayed and deeply disappointed by someone significant in his life. Whoever did the betrayal— parents, children, spouse, friend, relatives, or business partner—the executive was left feeling as if other people could not be trusted. In general, relationships seem like more work than they are worth, and as a result, one is just better off to depend only on oneself.

This executive fails to understand a key component of the human condition—shortcomings. He has shortcomings just like everyone else. But he doesn't usually see it this way. He expects others to be perfect, and when they fail to be perfect, it becomes one more piece of evidence that others are not to be trusted.

This creates a closed loop that the executive can't escape. He holds others to the standard of perfection and they let him down, every time. Rather than acknowledge humanness of failing, he chooses to withdraw from others, thinking this will diminish his disappointment—if he isn't dependent on others, they can't disappoint him.

With this executive, it's really helpful to think of the internal Child. He is just like a child, demanding that others act as he wants them to. When they don't, he does something analogous to stamping his feet and locking himself in his room. This, of course, only further alienates him and does nothing for achieving what he originally wanted. So he becomes angrier and more withdrawn.

He is, in essence, demanding that others love and care for him, and when they don't, it compounds his pain. Because his typical reaction to withdraw is driven by his Child, he never really learns how to approach others in a way that elicits the love and attention he needs. The more he withdraws, the less others provide what he wants.

Understanding the Life Script

The insight a coach guides the client with a crisis of isolation toward is this: His lifelong strategy for handling difficult situations is to withdraw. Withdrawal and isolation have been components of a lifelong script when things became painful. For example, when he didn't get the love and affection he needed as a child, he withdrew and became "a loner." When a spouse betrayed him, he refused to allow others close enough to hurt him. When a powerful boss betrayed his career, he retreated to lick his wounds and survived just long enough to make it to retirement, or the next good job opportunity, whichever came first.

As time went on and the executive became more practiced at the art of withdrawal, he would begin to withdraw even before the situation became difficult. When his previously happy marriage hit a few small bumps in the road, he began withdrawing, making the small problems into insurmountable ones. The same is true at work. When he would see the warning signs of a difficult project or committee, he would find an excuse to remove himself and return to something that seemed safer. His tendency to withdraw early makes the problem go from bad to worse much more quickly, and makes life more difficult for him.

For example, when a person can't make his mortgage payment, ignoring the situation only makes it worse (and hastens foreclosure). So it is with so many situations in life and work—withdrawal only makes the problems worse, not go away. He may ignore the declining profit numbers for months or quickly drop product lines that don't immediately show strong sales. All these actions, and many more, are forms of withdrawal. Anytime an executive disengages from a problem and tries to ignore it, he is withdrawing.

Recognizing the script of withdrawal is a powerful insight for the client. When all the pieces start to fall into place and the picture becomes clear, he sees what is happening to him and discovers that this crisis is really the culmination of a life script of withdrawing to avoid pain.

As with all the crises, the coach cannot provide the insight to the client—he can only guide the other person's exploration in the direction of insight. Even when the overeager coach "tells" the client the appropriate insight, it often is met with passive agreement or maybe even denial.

168

The coach must simply hold this critical insight in mind and ask probing questions that lead the client to discover the insight for himself. Useful questions, when asked at the appropriate time, include:

"It sounds like you spent a great deal of time alone as a child. What happened to that child?"

"After your divorce you mentioned that you became more cynical about human nature. How do you think that cynicism is affecting your life now?"

"When your boss used your ideas and didn't give you credit for them, you said you stopped offering your ideas. Is it possible that in some ways you are self-sabotaging your career?"

Once the client acknowledges the lifelong pattern of withdrawal, you're ready to move on to the behavioral practice that will help the client break the pattern.

Finding the Courage

The courage this executive needs to discover is to accept other people as flawed human beings. This means he must accept the inevitable fact that others will make mistakes and disappoint him. It doesn't mean that others aren't trustworthy—only that they are truly human.

Why does it take courage to accept the flaws of other people? Quite simply because you must accept yourself as flawed, too. You must accept your own shortcomings and weaknesses, in essence your "dark" side, if you are to be comfortable with these same things in other people. Very often the motive to withdraw is a defense mechanism aimed at repressing something about yourself you'd rather not face. In other words, when someone else does something hurtful, it forces you to acknowledge that you are capable of doing the same thing. If you are unwilling to find that same capability in yourself, you withdraw from the person.

It takes great courage for the abused child to stop blaming his parents and to accept them for who they are. For the adult child to do this, he must begin to see that given the right circumstances, he could be a child abuser, too. The same is true with a betrayed spouse. Once the betrayed accepts that he is capable of creating the same injury, he can begin to reestablish a relationship with the betrayer. Perhaps neither the abused child nor the betrayed spouse will choose to have the same abusive kind of relationship, but both can begin to deal with the offending person in a mature and healthy way.

The executive with a crisis of isolation discovers the courage he needs by, rather than blaming others for mistakes, taking the time to understand how such a mistake could have been made, and further how it is possible that in certain circumstances he might make the same mistake. Then, he stays engaged with the other person.

C A S E
S T U D Y

THE COURAGE TO MAKE AND ACCEPT MISTAKES

Dwight was the executive director of a nonprofit arts organization that managed a budget of over $2 million annually. The staff size had varied a great deal over the years, but one thing remained constant: Staff members rarely stayed for more than a year. Dwight inevitably discovered a shortcoming in every person who worked for him, and once he found this fault, he began to withdraw and become very parental. It didn't take long for employees to realize they had dropped out of favor with the executive director, and soon afterward they would move on to another job.

Dwight discovered the courage to embrace his own shortcomings and thereby the shortcomings of his employees in a few small steps. First, every time he found himself disapprovingly critical of an employee, he would sit down and write three reasons why he might have made the same mistake.

It was a simple, almost elementary exercise, but it worked. In a few months, Dwight was brimming with insight into his own behavior, to the point that he was even discussing his tendency to be too critical with his employees. The employees noticed a big change and began to see Dwight in a different light.

By taking a small action, Dwight found the courage to accept some of his own shortcomings and, consequently, the shortcomings of his employees. They weren't necessarily deep flaws, but just the ordinary mistakes, such as failing to proofread a letter or making a simple arithmetic error in accounting. Those were the little things that used to drive him crazy about an employee, but now he was less severe in his judgment. It took a great deal of courage to face the fact that he wasn't perfect and that it was extremely unfair of him to expect his employees to be perfect.

Confronting the Parent/Child Messages

There are usually two automatic Parent/Child messages associated with this crisis. Let us look at each of them.

I CAN'T TOLERATE OTHER PEOPLE'S MISTAKES

This automatic message is often the result of a child reacting to a strict and demanding parental figure. A child who is expected to grow up very quickly, and to fulfill the unfulfilled dreams of the parent, grows up under enormous pressure to be perfect. Even the smallest mistakes send the child into a panic. He must be the perfect child.

When that child becomes an executive, he carries in him both the Child and the unrelenting Parent. Inside, he is at war with himself. He must be perfect in everything he does; should he make a mistake, he makes himself suffer mercilessly for it. He continually flagellates, berates, and denies himself any pleasure.

Consequently, he can't tolerate other people's mistakes. He expects himself to be perfect and therefore expects the same of others. His Parent is demanding and unforgiving, saying in

171

essence to others: "I expect you to be perfect and if you're not, there will be hell to pay."

WORKING WITH OTHER PEOPLE IS OFTEN MORE TROUBLE THAN IT IS WORTH

As a consequence of expecting perfection from others, this executive is always let down and disappointed by others. Of course, they can't fulfill his rigid standards, and his Parent can't tolerate their mistakes. What does he do? He learns that it is often easier to do things himself than to involve other people. He trusts no one to do the job as he would do it.

This message often comes directly from the Parent. You can almost hear this executive's parental figure saying to him, "It looks like if I want the job done right, I better do it myself!" As a child, his hard work and diligence were met with disapproval because he wasn't perfect, and so the love and affection he was trying so hard to earn once again didn't come.

He doesn't enjoy punishing others for their imperfections because his memory is alive with how badly he felt when he wasn't perfect. Nonetheless, his Parent is relentlessly pushing him to expect perfection. The way he handles this internal conflict is to do the job himself rather than delegate it to others. That way, he doesn't have to punish someone else for not being perfect and the job gets done just the way he wants it.

PART
FOUR

THE
MOTIVATIONAL
CRISES

This section describes the crises that are characterized primarily by an executive's diminished motivation for the job. While each chapter describes a distinct crisis, it should be noted that in practice, an executive may have elements of several crises, including those discussed previously in Part Three on "The Relationship Crises."

TWELVE

THE CRISIS

OF PASSION

I had been the golden boy of the company. Everything I did seemed to turn out great and I raced up the corporate ladder. I heard it said that even the CEO had his eye on me. But where things went wrong, I'm not sure. All I know is I became unbelievably bored. Day in and day out it was same old grind.

It started to feel like I couldn't take it any more.

It was about this time that I had dinner with Trevor, one of our senior VPs, and his wife. When I arrived at his house, Trevor was standing in the entrance. He shook my hand and, taking my elbow, escorted me into the large, high-ceilinged living room—he had a truly beautiful home. This is where I first saw Mrs. Trevor. Standing near a low coffee table was one of the most striking women I had ever seen. She had long blonde hair, translucent skin, and deep blue eyes. Never before or since have I seen such a beautiful woman. Trevor must have been accustomed to the sensation his wife created when he said in his usual low and matter of fact voice, "This is my wife, Karen."

When I left dinner about 9:30 that evening, I stopped at an outdoor phone booth and called information for Trevor's number. When a feminine voice answered, I said, "May I speak with Karen?"

When Karen took the phone, I said, "This is Michael, Karen. Will you meet me privately tomorrow at 3:30 in the afternoon at Kon Tiki? I'll wait in the lounge. I need to talk over some important business with you."

And that's how the whole affair started. At first, it was just mid-afternoon meetings at some remote little place. Eventually, we started meeting at a motel just outside of town. I knew I was playing with my career. If Trevor ever found out, I'd be done for. But somehow, the thrill of it all kept me going. For almost six months we met at least once a week.

One afternoon before our usual staff meeting, I answered the phone and it was Karen on the line. "I told him," she said softly. "I'm sorry, Michael. I had to do it. I just couldn't go on like this. I told Trevor everything. I'm sorry . . .". I put down the receiver and that's when everything gets fuzzy. All I remember is walking into the staff meeting and seeing Trevor's face. I knew my career was over . . . .

Imagine waking up one morning to discover that you are a stranger in a foreign world. Everything is very familiar to you— where you live, who you live with, your job—but distinctly foreign, too. "What is this life?" you wonder. "How did I come to be this person?"

Without a doubt the crisis of passion is one of the most gut-wrenching and difficult crises that an executive can experience. The experience is like someone suddenly snapped you out of a trance and you discover that you have spent twenty (or thirty or forty) years creating a life that you never really dreamed of having. It's not that it's a bad life; it's more that it isn't the life you had intended to create for yourself way back when.

Of all the crises, this one is clearly the most existential, and as such is pervasive and devastating on many levels. The executive who is experiencing the crisis is likely to have difficulty expressing what is troubling him. After all, the life he is living is the life he has created for himself—so how can he now say that it isn't what he wants? It sounds crazy in his head and even crazier when he speaks it.

The crisis of passion isn't about broken dreams; it's about *lost* dreams: What happened to the dream of becoming a football coach? Did you really want to become a facilities manager instead? What happened to the dream of owning your own business? When did you decide that you'd be happier being a corporate drone instead? Weren't you the one who was going to write a best-selling novel? At what point did you decide that writing strategic business plans was more interesting and fulfilling?

To understand what the crisis of passion is all about, you have to grasp the essence of passion and its centrality in a fulfilled life. No one can define passion—it is an idiosyncratic experience of what really excites you and turns you on. What's more, passion is organic and flowing, changing with the seasons of your life. What you are passionate about today isn't what you'll passionate about five years from now. Passion is a journey, a life stream, and a constant discovery.

Herein lies the trouble with passion. If you want passion in your life, you must follow it wherever it leads you. As your passion changes, you must change the course of your life's trajectory. Sometimes, however, where your passion leads you isn't where the organizational strategic initiatives direct, and you're faced with a difficult decision. Do you follow your passion or follow the plan? Do you take the high-paid promotion or demote yourself into a position that excites you?

Quite understandably, many executives left their passion at the door to their career. They wanted success and to climb the corporate ladder. They were willing to be great employees in exchange for a seat at the table. "Give me the opportunity," the executive says, "and I'll show you how great a job I can do."

And for the first years, even decades of their careers, the challenge of proving themselves was enough. There were promotions and transfers, new jobs and more responsibility, all keeping them busy and feeling as if they were moving forward.

Then one day, who knows what traumatic or insignificant event triggers it, something reminds them of their long-lost passion. They remember the days when they cared about something and wanted to make a difference. They are flooded with the lost feelings of passionate inspiration. Suddenly, the promotions, titles, and corner offices don't mean one damn thing.

I Just Want to Feel Inspired

The crisis passion is one of the most painful experiences of an executive's lifetime. If the crisis remains unresolved, it can destroy careers, marriages, and virtually everything the executive has worked for throughout his life.

Why is this crisis so destructive? Because nothing that he has worked for means very much to him now. It all reminds him of how he sold his soul and abandoned his passion.

In severe cases, the crisis of passion should be treated by both a coach and a therapist. Because it can sometimes be accompanied by depression and other clinical maladies, a therapist can be of great assistance. In a few extreme cases, suicidal thoughts may be present. When this happens, the coach must immediately refer the executive to a competent mental health professional.

The reason this crisis can feel so dire is because it invalidates many years of hard work and struggle. The realization that you have worked most of your life for something that you may not even want is devastating.

The pain of the crisis is deepened by the fact that the executive can't just make a decision and fix the problem. He can't just switch jobs or start writing the long-put-off novel. It's far more complex than that. He doesn't know what his passion is anymore.

So many years of trading off his passion for the kudos and rewards of a corporate career have left him without a sense of what really inspires him. Passion is a cultivated experience—the more one experiences and follows his passion, the more of it he feels. Likewise, years of denying passion leave one without the ability to feel much passion at all. All that is left is the memory of a dream.

During the height of this crisis, the executive may believe that almost everything is futile and meaningless. He may continue to go through the motions, but the energy with which he once attacked his work is gone. In essence, he begins to tread water.

It Must Be a Midlife Crisis

Almost overnight, someone who was once a dependable, hard-working executive has started acting strangely. He doesn't seem to have to the edge he once had, and the force he once brought to the job is gone.

It some cases it may look like what is sometimes called a "midlife crisis." Maybe he left his wife and bought a sports car. Maybe he even quit a lucrative job on the spot. Maybe he just started coming to work late and leaving early.

When an executive coach is called in, it's usually because this executive has "stalled" on the job. He shies away from new initiatives that might take energy and investment on his part and instead chooses to maintain the status quo, hoping that he can just get by until he figures things out for himself. He adopts a distinctly more cynical view of his peers and the organization. In short, he seems tired, bored, and maybe even a bit anxious.

Burnt Out

A sure sign of a crisis of passion is burnout or boredom. Executives who are passionate about their jobs don't get burnout—they get tired, maybe even exhausted, but not burnt out.

Think about some of the most successful and satisfied executives you know. Chances are they are constantly on the go, but never seem to tire of it. Their work could be called hectic and stressful by some, but they see it differently. A hard day's work seems to give them some sort of psychic boost, not drain them.

Why don't these executives get burnt out? It's really quite simple: They're doing what they love. Even though it is demanding, tiring, and fast-paced, they love it, and it is the love of their work that sustains them.

Sam Walton, the legendary founder of Wal-Mart, kept what some would call a grueling schedule of visiting Wal-Mart stores around the country. It wasn't grueling to Sam; he loved to visit the stores, and when he attended a store meeting it usually turned into a pep rally. He was passionate about selling, and the stores were where it all happened. Several times a week (up until a few weeks before his death) he would pilot his own plane across the country, visiting the stores where he knew many of the salespeople by name.

If he didn't really have a passion for selling, Sam's job would have chewed him up in no time. But because he loved what he did, it energized him instead of draining him. That's what passion is all about. So when an executive finds himself burnt out, run down, or bored by the job, there's a good chance that somewhere along the road he's lost touch with his passion.

The Wrong Path

Another component of the crisis of passion is that an executive never really had an opportunity to explore his passion. Think about it. How old were you when you decided what college to attend, what your major would be, or what job to take after graduation? For most of us, those were tumultuous years of self-discovery. Everything was so new, including our emancipation from parental control. We'd never worked at a real job, and yet we made some crucial decisions that affected the rest of our careers.

So it was for most executives. To make matters worse, executives often invest further in their career choices with post-graduate degrees and resume-building jobs that the company encourages them to pursue. It is the logical progression of a mis-informed career choice.

Now, years later, they are fully invested in a career that isn't meaningful and doesn't satisfy the urge within themselves to feel inspired. They've done all the right things, but unfortunately, they left their passion behind in the process.

It's Not Me—It's Those Jerks I Work With

In every crisis the temptation is strong for the executive to blame it on the people around him, but in this crisis it is espe-cially strong. It seems easier to pin his own dissatisfaction with work on someone else than to admit he's created his own prob-lems. Blaming others for our own faults is a fairly common human reaction.

CASE STUDY

"IT'S EVERYONE ELSE'S PROBLEM"

Arlene is a minister who was recently hired by a church that was languishing. Several previous ministers hadn't been ter-ribly popular with the congregation and attendance had begun to shrink. Arlene had said all the right words in her interviews and impressed the congregation with her sermon delivery and operatic singing voice. Unfortunately for the church, what she didn't say was that she really didn't have a passion for ministry. She wasn't fond of visiting the sick, she found inspirations for sermons difficult to come by, and she was growing increasingly depressed. She had spent years training for the ministry, but once the newness of it all had worn off, she discovered she didn't like it very much.

Not surprisingly, attendance at the church continued to drop off. Arlene's sermons seemed increasingly stiff and dispirited. The congregation began to wonder what had happened to the seemingly dynamic person they had hired only six months earlier. In time, the revenue of the church declined to the point that all the office staff had to be laid off and expenses were cut back severely.

Arlene's response to the decline in attendance was to blame the congregation's commitment to attending church. When the board of directors approached her on the subject, she angrily reminded them that they weren't doing well before she arrived, so there must be something wrong with the church. They just weren't ready for her style of ministry, she claimed.

It can be painful to admit that you've lost touch with your passion, and so it was for Arlene. Instead of looking inside herself and admitting that she had lost inspiration, she struck out at the people around her. Arlene's response isn't that unusual. "It's not me who isn't inspired," she seemed to say, "it's the people I work with."

The Fear Complex

What causes the crisis of passion is the fear of one's own feelings. When an executive is willing to abandon his most treasured dreams for himself and follow someone else's direction for his career, there is something tragically wrong with his deepest feelings about himself. Somewhere he learned not to trust his feelings and came to accept that others knew better how he should live his life.

The essence of this fear complex is that he believes there is something wrong, evil, or misguided about his feelings and therefore he believes he can't trust them. This is a serious and extremely damaging fear that causes him to literally abandon his own desires for something that he believes can be trusted. All too often, this executive chooses to follow the conventional road to corporate success by following the path his superiors ask him to follow. Success, as defined by a corporate culture, is what he trades his passion for.

That success, sadly, doesn't satisfy him because it isn't success that is elicited by his passion. For example, if I were to attain success as a gourmet chef, it might feel good for a while, but since cooking isn't my passion, it would ultimately mean very little to me. Becoming a gourmet chef isn't my dream for my life. In fact, if I were to spend the majority of my career trying to become an accomplished chef, I would eventually be left with the feeling that my life was something of a waste. Why? Because I never yearned to become a chef, and hence, that accomplishment won't satisfy my craving for fulfilled passion.

To take this example one step further, imagine that I became a chef because my father was a world-renowned chef who owned several restaurants and wanted me to join him in his business. If I didn't really trust my feelings to guide me (i.e., my feelings of wanting to become something other than a chef), it would be extremely difficult for me not to join my father's business. After all, it would seem foolish for me to pass up such a wonderful financial opportunity—excepting the fact that it isn't my passion.

The executive must *first* follow his passion and then be responsible and keep his commitments. Obligations, responsibilities, and commitments are no substitute for following one's passion. That's definitely a case of the tail wagging the dog.

Not trusting his feelings is likely to be the result of years of training and denial for this executive. Chances are good that he's been doing it for most of his life. One important way that many executives abandon their passion is by trying to live their parents' unlived dreams. Maybe his father always wanted to be an executive, but never had the chance to go to college. Or maybe his mother always wanted to travel, and now he has the money to travel the globe.

It is often extremely insightful for an executive with a crisis of passion to explore the ways in which he may have tried to live his parents' unlived dreams. Here's what a few clients have told me:

❖ I was supposed to grow up and be a wealthy lawyer who in his spare time coached the high school football team— two things my father always wished he had done. Well,

I've done exactly that and it doesn't really mean a thing to me. I'm head of the legal department at my company and have coached six seasons of football at my son's school. Now, all I really want to do is quit, buy a small sailboat, and spend my days sailing around the Caribbean.

❖ My parents always wanted a child to graduate from Harvard Business School. Why, I can't say, but ever since I was young I remember them saying to me, "You're going to be the one that will make us proud." My brothers weren't much for the books and didn't attend college, so my parents pinned all their hopes on me. I really didn't have any choice.

❖ My real dream after college was to be, of all things, a foreign correspondent in South America. I spent summers there during college and learned Spanish and Portuguese fluently. I'd visited almost every country at least one time and been in several of the most remote mountain villages. I loved every minute of it. My parents were Holocaust survivors, and they felt strongly that I should pursue something more secure and safe. "Why would you want to traipse across poor countries making peanuts?" my father would ask. "I didn't pay for that expensive education so you could waste it! If only I'd had the opportunities in this country that you have," he'd yell, throwing his hands in the air. I didn't want to be an ungrateful son; after all, they'd been through so much. So I started at the bottom with the best company I could find, Procter & Gamble, and after a few false starts and jobs at other companies, I worked my way to the top of this one.

❖ Do you know what it's like to grow up in Puerto Rico? All my friends from back in high school are hourly workers or tradesmen if they're lucky. My parents had a little money, and I had an uncle in New York who wanted to help me out. So I left the island for college and ended up in New Jersey. I've been here for twenty years and hate it.

I always wonder what was so important about leaving such a beautiful island. Maybe it isn't so bad to be a tradesman . . . and happy?

Understanding the Life Script

As we seen, the life script that creates this crisis is usually one that is laced with denial and suppression of feelings. The basic tenet of the script is: "I can't trust my feelings. They are a bad influence and will lead me astray."

Not long ago, I encountered an executive who told me that one of the guiding principles of his career was to never let his emotions get the best of him. Ironically, he remembers being given that same advice when he was much younger and considering buying a small house in Hawaii as a vacation home. His father told him, "Don't let your emotions get the best of you!" Believing this, he decided the purchase was frivolous and emotional, so he passed. "Do you have any idea how much that house would be worth today, not to mention how much enjoyment it would have brought me?"

The life script of this executive has been one that saw emotions as a weakness that should be compensated for by intellect. Instead of feeling, he intellectualized. Whenever traumatic events happened, such as the loss of parent, or the breakup of relationship, he forced himself to be strong and unemotional about it. When he spoke to friends and family about what had happened, he did so with a detachment that seemed as if he were telling a story about what happened to someone else.

He may also be preoccupied with the "right thing to do" in most any situation. Since he can't trust the internal guidance of his feelings, he must consult with external rules and values about what is good and right. It may be religious-based, but not necessarily. Many executives obsess on the rule that "only something that makes money is good." Because many of the things in life that are truly meaningful don't make a dime, this executive misses out on a great deal. He's bound to do the right thing—not necessarily the thing that *feels* right.

Finding the Courage

To resolve the crisis, this executive needs the courage to begin to explore and honor his feelings. A great way to facilitate this self-discovery is to encourage the executive to try to adopt a new model of behavior. The old model looked like this:

1. Disregard your feelings.
2. Think.
3. Act.

The new model is quite different:

1. Feel.
2. Think.
3. Act.

The coach encourages this executive to consciously ask himself, "What do I feel about this?" before trying to intellectually sort out the situation. You're asking him to first consider what he feels and then think through the facts. By doing this, the executive becomes less uncomfortable with his feelings, knowing that they won't necessarily control him—you're not asking him to abandon his intellect, only to first consider his feelings.

It can be very helpful to couple this activity with a homework assignment of journalizing his feelings. Every day, ask him to write a page or two about what he is feeling about the events of the day. Be careful. It's extraordinarily easy for him to slip back into the mode of intellectualizing his feelings. You're not asking for problem analysis, you're asking him for his feelings. This process can be facilitated by insisting that he use as many sentences beginning with "I feel . . ." as he can.

Another helpful way to build the courage to discover feelings is to encourage your client to pursue activities that are outside of his comfort zone. Chances are, he's structured his life so that nothing evokes strong feelings. By encouraging him to pursue activities that are outside of what he normally does, he is likely to stumble across some very powerful feelings. Has he always wanted

186

to go on an African safari? Has he wanted to take mountain-climbing lessons? Has he wanted to start his own company? Has he wanted to oversee a new product that he has designed? Whatever the activity, encourage him to dive into it. There's nothing better to jump-start a person's feelings than taking action.

Confronting the Parent/Child Messages

It is also vital for the executive experiencing a crisis of passion to acknowledge and examine the Parent/Child messages that have contributed to his dilemma. These statements become automatic and self-defeating.

I SHOULDN'T GET CARRIED AWAY

This automatic statement is merely a veiled restatement of the fear of feelings. "Getting carried away" means acting on your feelings. By telling himself that he shouldn't get carried away, he is actually telling himself not to let his feelings influence his actions.

SOMETIMES YOU DON'T GET WHAT YOU WANT

This statement comes from the deprived or abandoned Child. I remember my grandfather saying that when he was a child, his family was extremely poor. When Christmas came around, he never got his hopes up too high. If he did, then he would just be disappointed and it would ruin Christmas. This is exactly what this automatic statement is telling the executive: Don't allow yourself to feel and desire because you'll be disappointed. In other words, to avoid the pain of not getting what you want, you stop wanting very much.

Helping people break the years-long habit of convincing themselves that they shouldn't want very much can be a challenge for the coach. Sometimes it's helpful to ask the executive to remember what he wanted his life to become when he was a child. By accessing those distant memories, you can often find the trail of emotion that has been covered by years of neglect and abandonment.

MY OBLIGATIONS COME FIRST

There is a very strong feeling among some executives that

responsible behavior requires one to abandon one's passion. In this executive's mind, it isn't possible to do what he really loves *and* meet his corporate, financial, and familial obligations. It's either one way or the other: You're irresponsible and passionate, or you're responsible, stable, and dispassionate.

Coaching requires that you challenge this false dichotomy. This automatic statement often goes back to other times and places, such as during the Great Depression, when it was very difficult to make a living, much less make a living at something you loved to do. During those times, passion was a luxury. Today's executives often have this statement stored in their Parent as a direct result of their parents' and grandparents' experiences: "The most important thing is to earn a good living and make yourself financially secure."

Times are different now. It is quite possible with the diversity of organizations and working styles for an executive to fashion his career in almost any way imaginable. He can live just about anywhere and find a company that does just about anything he wants to do. Not only is it possible for him to follow his passion, it's necessary if he wants the fullest life possible. Who among us doesn't crave that?

THIRTEEN

THE CRISIS OF COMMITMENT

My day starts at 6:00 a.m. when I start the hour-long commute to the office. Once I'm on the freeway, I check voice mail using my cell phone. I arrive at the office by 7:00 a.m. and usually have my first meeting of the day by 7:30. It isn't unusual at all for me to be in one meeting after another until mid-afternoon. Every now and then I find a few hours in the afternoon to think about the department and my plans for the future, but that's rare.

Being a corporate executive requires a person to multitask more than is humanly possible . . . but you've got to try anyway. I never have time to focus on any one project before I'm racing off to another meeting. Luckily I've got a great secretary and a dynamite staff to follow up for me. Without them, I'd be sunk.

My boss is always pushing me to spend more time on this or that project, but I tell him I just don't have the time. I've got so many balls in the air, I can't pause without everything falling apart.

Busy. Friendly. Attends the right meetings. Talks the talk. This is likely to be your first impression of the executive who has a crisis of commitment. On the surface, everything looks just fine.

But look a little deeper and what you'll find is the executive who fills his day with busyness and keeps a hand in many pots, but lacks any serious focus. He may even complain of his hectic schedule and the tedious demands of his job, but when forced to talk about what he has actually produced, it usually boils down to attending lots of meetings, having lots of conversations, and doing what is required to keep the doors open and the employees paid. The truth is that he refuses to take control of his schedule so he can focus on any one project. Instead, he allows himself to be pushed and pulled in many different directions.

Whereas the crisis of passion is the most visible and painful of the executive crises, the crisis of commitment is probably the subtlest. These executives "pass" as hardworking, motivated executives, but actually they are masters at dodging commitments that may require them to put their own competence on the line.

C A S E
S T U D Y

TALKING THE TALK, BUT DODGING THE COMMITMENTS

Marty was a typical executive with a crisis of commitment. She was the director of communications for a large retail organization that had nearly 500 stores nationwide. Marty was friendly, organized, and definitely looked the part of a successful executive. Marty's calendar was often full for weeks at time with various meetings and committees she participated on throughout the company. In addition, Marty regularly flew across the country to visit staff members that she had located in the five regional distribution centers. By all indications, Marty seemed like an executive on the rise.

As I began to work with Marty (I worked with the organization as a consultant, not as Marty's coach), I observed that all her peers throughout the company held her in high regard and commented on how busy she was, although none could really tell me what she did. As I began to investigate further, I discovered something very interesting. Marty talked a good game. She could talk about all the important projects around the company in detail, and readily implied her involvement in all the details of the work.

In reality, Marty wasn't really accomplishing much. "I'm so busy with the stores' reorganization," she would tell the buyers' selection committee, "I can't spare the time to interview the new candidates." Since the buyers' selection committee members weren't familiar with the stores' reorganization project, they'd divide the work so that Marty got the lightest load. She did this repeatedly, playing one division against another in ways that were unlikely to be discovered.

Of the projects she was directly responsible for, most were being completed by outside consultants who needed very little supervision. To hear Marty talk, you'd think she was

191

doing every bit of the work herself, but it turns out that just wasn't the case.

To completely understand Marty's crisis, you need to know that several years before, Marty had been the primary executive in charge of creating a "branch" of corporate headquarters in Texas (the main headquarters was in California). She was deeply involved in the project and spent the better portion of two years working to make it happen. Unfortunately, decisions that were made by the parent company interfered with the creation of the branch headquarters and the project was dropped.

Marty's disappointment extended beyond just the lost time and effort. Her dream had been to eventually move to the women's sportswear division from the communications department that she ran. One of the promises that had been made to her was that a position in women's sportswear would be created in the branch headquarters that would be a lateral move, allowing her to transfer without losing any salary or status in the organization. The failure of the project destroyed the possibility of her transferring.

After that debacle, Marty became reluctant to commit to any other projects. Of course, she couldn't directly refuse (that would have had serious, negative consequences to her career), so she began the pattern of dodging possible commitments. Soon she realized that as long as she kept abreast of what was happening throughout the company, she could use that information to avoid extra work.

I'm Too Busy to Focus

The executive in a crisis of commitment often feels dissatisfied and harried. The ongoing burden of "looking busy" is tiring and offers little fulfillment. Since this executive may not be aware of his own avoidance tactics, he may also be resentful that other executives are receiving more of the spotlight than he is. "Why are they getting all the promotions and bonuses?" he might wonder.

This executive has come to confuse the process of work with the work itself. For example, meetings become results rather than vehicles for producing results. The tasks of booking and attending meetings, scheduling staff one-on-one meetings, writing internal memos, and so on become the only product this executive produces. When he talks about what he has accomplished, he is likely to point to many of these "process" events rather than any tangible accomplishment.

He's Always Busy, But What Does He Do?

Reaction to an executive with a crisis of commitment is likely to vary, depending on how much someone must rely on the executive to produce. From a distance, this executive may actually earn the respect and admiration of others for his incredible schedule. For those who must rely on the executive to produce, the experience can be entirely different.

CASE STUDY

NO FOLLOW-UP

Terry is a human resources manager at a high-tech company. He is handsome, smart, and well educated. One colleague said of Terry, "He can charm the birds right out of the tree if he wants to!"

I first worked closely with Terry when we were both officers for a professional association. Terry had been elected president of the association, which was a prominent position in the field of human resources.

Very quickly the staff of the association and fellow officers, including myself, had to make some important decisions regarding next year's convention. A city had to be chosen, hotel rooms reserved, and speakers booked. There must have been a few thousand details that needed to be tended to within our first months as officers.

The hired staff of the association looked to Terry for answers to many of these questions, but was frustrated with his non-committal response. Terry would usually tell the staff to wait until the next board meeting so that all the officers could decide the issue, or he'd refer the staff to one of the other officers.

For even small issues, I noticed that it was terribly difficult to get Terry on the phone. Whenever I'd call his office, his secretary would say that he was in a meeting, or unavailable, and then take a message. Rarely would I hear back from Terry, and then only if I said the issue was absolutely urgent.

As the weeks dragged into months, very few of the decisions were being made for the conference. Since the board of officers only met every three months, most of the important issues were waiting for our next meeting—but by then it would be too late for many of them. Finally, the executive director called several of the officers regarding the difficulty she was having getting Terry to make decisions. She was in a very delicate place since technically Terry was her boss and she was noticeably careful about what she said.

When one of the officers called and spoke with Terry about the issue (we all lived in different cities), he was his usual charming self. He said that he thought the board should be making these decisions as a group, and furthermore, he didn't have time to be making "all the decisions." He was going out of the country and really wouldn't be available until the next board meeting, so the rest of the officers would have to fill in for him anyway.

Ultimately, we all pitched in and made arrangements for the conference just before several critical deadlines passed. The next year at the conference, Terry presided as president and took full credit for the success of the association that year and the conference.

In the years that followed, I was to work with many of Terry's colleagues from the companies where he had worked. Almost everyone who worked closely with him reported the same experience we had at the association; namely, Terry was an excellent speaker and meeting leader but rarely followed up with the details. Fortunately for him, he usually had a staff who would clean up after him and keep him looking good.

The Safety Net

The executive with a crisis of commitment usually develops a knack for hiring a staff to cover for him. They are usually very competent and willing to do the work he leaves undone. He expects his staff to take care of the details, and because they do, he is able to survive.

Of course, the staff usually becomes bitter when they are doing their boss's job and making the decisions he isn't willing to make. They often move on to other jobs. So ironically, the executive feels it is hard to find a staff that he can depend on. There is a genuine disconnect here—he refuses to commit to work, but fully expects his staff to be hardworking and dependable.

A Little Wiggle Room, Please!

This executive is usually great at using language that is trendy but meaningless. For example, he may talk about getting feedback, or evaluating a project, but never in specific terms. His conversations and agreements are usually fuzzy and leave plenty of wiggle room.

As you can imagine, there is often a strong distaste with this executive for measurable outcomes. He'll say things like, "You can't show quality in a number" and "The numbers don't tell the whole story." Quantification of results pins him down in a way that is difficult to escape. He'd rather tell stories and anecdotes about the outcome than measure it.

The Filibuster

Another tactic of the executive with a crisis of commitment can be the filibuster. An effective filibuster is one that is on a topic that is relatively agreeable and is spoken eloquently enough so that the audience can't interrupt. And, of course, the filibuster is designed to be long enough to prevent making a decision.

When the executive perceives in a meeting that he is about to be assigned certain responsibilities, this is the perfect time for a filibuster. He begins talking, raising new issues, and generally clouding the issue so no decision can be made. By the time he is finished, everyone is cross-eyed with exhaustion and overload. If the executive has been effective, he escapes the meeting without any new commitments.

At one senior executive meeting, the executive in charge of customer service was about to be charged with conducting a large-scale survey of the company's customers. Not wanting that commitment, he launched into his filibuster. Here's what his colleague had to say about it later:

> They were all nodding and agreeing, but I could see we were just wasting our time. No one wanted to be the one to tell him he was blowing hot air, so they just sat and listened to him ramble on. After all, no one could disagree with the fact that we needed to act more like a team. But wasting all this time talking about our values and mission didn't solve the problem. Everyone walked out of that meeting and went right back to doing the same old thing.

Putting It to Paper

Another distinctive characteristic of the executive with a crisis of commitment is a difficulty in putting anything on paper. Written words carry much more of a commitment than do spoken words, and consequently he struggles with writing. Whether it's a letter to a customer, a memo to his boss, or a catalog description of a product, he pours over the words, writing and rewriting many times before he submits the final document.

C A S E
S T U D Y

CAN'T COMMIT TO PAPER

Jillian was the head of a small division within a larger medical conglomerate. One of her duties was to produce a strategic plan every three years. This particular year was when Jillian's first plan was due. She labored over the plan, hiring a consultant to help her structure it and review everything she wrote. She wrote, rewrote, submitted it to the consultant, and rewrote what the consultant wrote. This went on for six months, during which time she did little else. After six months, she presented the document to her staff and asked for their suggestions, most of which she found a way to incorporate into the plan during the following month of rewriting. Finally, when the due date came, Jillian was forced to turn in the plan, but did so only after she had spent nearly a week of sleepless nights revising the text.

On the day that she presented her plan to the corporate executive committee, their response was almost unanimous. While the document was thorough and even verbose, there wasn't any new action in the plan. All of the nearly 300 objectives were simply descriptive of what the division was already doing. The committee sent Jillian back to revise the plan and make it more aggressive and strategic. Frustrated and angry at their response, Jillian eventually quit the organization to become the executive director of a local nonprofit organization.

I've discovered that Jillian's experience is typical of an executive with a commitment crisis. She was terrified of writing assignments and the commitment they required of her. It was one thing for her to suggest that her division would accomplish a particular goal, but quite another to commit to it on paper. Spoken words could be spun and revised if needed; written words left precious little wiggle room.

The Fear Complex

What lies at the bottom of the crisis of commitment is a fear complex of failure. If an executive doesn't commit to a task, then he can't fail at it. He can't lose a race that he doesn't enter.

You can't fail at something you don't try. For example, you can't become a "washed-up artist" if you never allow yourself to make paintings. Similarly, you can't become a bankrupt entrepreneur if don't allow yourself to start a business. By anticipating possible failure, the executive with a crisis of commitment avoids any situation where he might fail, and in so doing, also eliminates many situations were he might be very successful. He sticks with the mediocre. That is safe and secure.

The fear complex of failure usually occurs when an executive has experienced extreme consequences for a failure. Often, this experience extends into childhood, but not always. Perhaps he failed a grade in school and was held back a year, making him the target of all the other children's jokes. Or perhaps he made a thoughtless error in a job that caused great expense, and as a result, he was fired. Whatever the failure, the consequences were so painful that it instilled a fear of failing again.

Psychologist Martin Seligman has demonstrated through numerous experiments and case studies that extreme consequences often produce a syndrome that he calls "learned helplessness." When punishment is great and repeated over time, a person begins to feel helpless and will stop trying to escape. The fear of the punishment paralyzes him, and he no longer can act assertively to change the situation.

Sometimes the fear complex of failure can create learned helplessness in an executive. When he is placed in an impossible job where nothing he does can possibly make a difference, he eventually becomes paralyzed and stops trying. Later, in other situations, he takes this feeling with him. Just as soon as a situation shows the potential for failure, he becomes paralyzed, imagining that once again nothing he does will make a difference.

The fear complex of failure creates a self-fulfilling cycle that can be difficult to break. By avoiding situations where there is possibility of failure, the executive doesn't actively fail, therefore reinforcing his belief that avoiding failure at all costs is a good thing. Each time he avoids potential failure, the more convinced he becomes that he is doing the right thing.

Of course, avoiding any potential failure will ultimately cause an executive to fail, if for no other reason than he becomes extremely adverse to risk. The more unwilling he becomes to take risk, the less he is able to accomplish. Consequently, he fails for lack of achieving anything of merit.

Often it is at the point of total risk aversion that the executive with a crisis of commitment comes for coaching. He will seem confused and angry, maybe even a bit paranoid. What he hasn't been able to see is that his extreme avoidance behavior has actually created what he sought to avoid.

Understanding the Life Script

The insight that coaching works toward with an executive in a crisis of commitment is this: Failure is a part of living and being human. It cannot be avoided.

Whatever the painful consequences were for his past failure, he must begin to see that he isn't helpless and can minimize the chances of failure without using his extreme avoidance tactics. Furthermore, the client must begin to see that failure can be instructive and isn't always punished. Many times, failure is simply the result of events that are not in his control.

One of the hidden truths about life is that failure is a part of every success. Somehow we imagine that successful people go through life with a million-dollar smile and a continual thumbs-up attitude. Not so. In fact, most of the world's most successful people have failed miserably more than once on the road to their greatest achievements. The proof is everywhere you see success:

❖ Brooks Robinson, called the greatest third baseman of all times, was sent back to the minors after a disappointing first year in the majors.

❖ Howard Head, the inventor who revolutionized the sports of skiing and tennis, spent more than five years trying to make a pair of metal skis that couldn't be broken. He made forty handmade pairs that failed before he finally reached his goal.

❖ The enormously profitable television show *Baywatch* was

canceled after its first season. Only after David Hasselhoff, an actor whose career had plummeted during the decade prior to *Baywatch*, bought the rights to the show did it find a market with a European syndicate and go on to be one of the most-watched shows in television history.

❖ Ted Koppel, the venerable newscaster of *Nightline*, spent years trying to get a job as a television news correspondent without any luck.

❖ Katie Couric, now a morning fixture at NBC's *Today Show*, was once told by the president of CNN that he never wanted to see her on camera again.

Of course, this principle of failure before success isn't just true of entertainment and television personalities. It is even more true of today's top executives:

❖ Lee Iacocca was fired from Ford Motor Company by Henry Ford II after a number of ambitious projects ultimately failed. He later found employment with Chrysler Motors, which was at the time virtually bankrupt. Iacocca returned the company to profitability in what is widely considered one of the greatest corporate "turnarounds" of all time.

❖ Lou Gerstner, CEO of IBM Corp., had been passed over for top positions at American Express and United Airlines because the boards of directors of those companies didn't have enough confidence in his ability to lead.

❖ Tom Monaghan, founder and former CEO of Domino's Pizza, drove the company into financial insolvency twice with bad business decisions. At one point, he was forced to hand over controlled interest in the company to a creditor. Years later, Tom regained control of 97 percent of the company and became one of the wealthiest entrepreneurs in the world.

Helping the executive to realize that failure can't be avoided is one of the most powerful insights he can achieve. It isn't that he fails that is important—it's what he does with the failure. If it shuts him down and steals his motivation, then it is truly a failure. It he learns from it and refuses to allow the failure to steal his dream, it becomes a stepping-stone in his career.

Finding the Courage

The executive with a crisis of commitment needs to discover the courage to embrace his weaknesses so that he no longer hides behind a façade of busyness. It's tough for him to acknowledge his weaknesses, but as long as he continues to deny them, he will be forced to avoid situations where those weaknesses might become visible. He can't fail, for that would reveal to the world what he refuses to acknowledge in himself.

A big part of the fear of one's weaknesses is an obsession with trying to fix oneself. Many executives attempt to avoid all failure by following all the latest management fads and seminars. But try as they may, they rarely improve. Those who don't have strong "people skills" rarely improve that weakness by attending the latest course on "managing relationships" or "dealing with difficult people." And those who have trouble managing their time don't do much better after time management training. It's not a popular thing to say, given all the money that is pumped into executive training, but it's something we all know is true ourselves: Certain long-standing weaknesses rarely improve no matter what we do.

The secret to resolving the crisis of commitment is to have the courage to face and embrace one's shortcomings, thereby defusing them of power. As long as you know what you don't do best, you can find any number of ways to prevent your weaknesses from harming you. But you can't protect yourself from what you don't know or won't acknowledge.

Confronting the Parent/Child Messages

Two of the more prominent Parent/Child messages that emerge

from this crisis are learned when the Child observes the Parent's behavior in dealing with commitment.

IF I DON'T GET TOO INVOLVED, NO ONE WILL DISCOVER MY WEAKNESSES

Failure to commit only creates another set problems for the executive. Sure, others may be less able to discover the limits of the executive's talent if he doesn't get too involved in any one project, but it also creates animosity and mistrust on the part of others. They quickly learn that the executive cannot be counted on to get a job done, so they do what they must to get around him. In the final analysis, the executive who can produce goes much further than the one who has potential to produce but never does.

AS LONG AS I'M NOT COMMITTED, I AM MORE IN CONTROL OF MY LIFE

The fear of commitment is closely allied with the fear of losing control. Once a person commits to something, whether it is a work project or a marriage, the person must give up some measure of control over his life. Project meetings are scheduled, and he is expected to attend. Dinner plans are made, and he is expected to be there.

There is no doubt that commitment involves relinquishing some control over your life. This is a hard truth for some to accept, but it is a basic truth of human nature.

The problem of not committing, however, doesn't necessarily increase one's control over life. For example, the high school student who can't commit to course work and graduate has less control, not more, over his future. The same is true about working in the corporate world. Being resistant to commitment doesn't increase an executive's control over his career. In fact, in many ways it decreases control.

Imagine the executive who takes on an ambitious project, learns everything he can about it, and then completes the project successfully. What's next for him? Perhaps a promotion. Perhaps he becomes an expert in that kind of project within the company. Perhaps competitors hear of his success and try to lure him away with a better position. The truth is, creating a track record of success only gives you more career options, which ultimately translates into more control over your life and career.

FOURTEEN

THE CRISIS
OF SELF-
CONFIDENCE

A construction developer had this to say about his crisis of self-confidence:

> I was on the verge of getting the biggest commission of my career and my anxiety shot through the roof—because this project would have lifted me to a level

203

of fame beyond anything I could have imagined. I hadn't taken a drink in three years, so I told myself it was okay to have one drink—to celebrate. I ended up smashed, insulted my client, and lost the project. My partner became so enraged at what I had done that he quit and started his own firm. I was devastated, but I was back in safe territory again, struggling to rise but not yet breaking through. I'm comfortable there.

The owner of a small chain of stores spoke of her own crisis this way:

I was determined not to be stopped by my husband or anyone else. I did not fault my husband because he earned less than I did, and I would not allow him to fault me for earning more than him. But there was this voice inside of me saying I was not supposed to be this successful and that I didn't deserve it. I became careless—neglecting important phone calls, treating customers rudely, and so on. At one point I lost my temper with my best buyer right there in one of the best restaurants in town . . . she was so humiliated that she walked out and never came back to work. The business suffered terribly and now I'm trying to build it back up.

Finally, a corporate executive had this to say:

I was in line for a promotion I had wanted for a long time. My life was in perfect order—a good marriage, smart kids, and I was making good money. Then all of a sudden I woke up in the night thinking I was having a heart attack, but the doctor said it was just anxiety. I guess I became so worried about the promotion and feeling like I didn't deserve it all that the anxiety kept building. Then I did something really stupid. I made a pass at the wife of one of my bosses during an office party. It was clumsy and thoughtless, and I knew who she was right from the beginning. I was certain I would be fired. As it turns out, I didn't get the promotion and all my anxiety has died down.

The common element in each of these stories is self-sabotage. Whenever you see someone who would otherwise be successful do something stupid—perhaps even intentional—to destroy his own success, it usually because of the crisis of self-confidence. He doesn't believe he deserves success, it makes him feel uncomfortable and out of place, so he consciously, or unconsciously, sabotages himself.

A surprisingly large number of executives suffer from a crisis of self-confidence, sometimes also called "the imposter syndrome." They can't believe their own success—it feels false to them and they imagine themselves to be imposters acting out the part of successful executives. When that crisis becomes inflamed, they act on these feelings and knock themselves back down to a level where they are comfortable. In essence they are balancing the equation: reducing their accomplishments to equal their low self-confidence.

I once had a coaching client who had just received a very nice promotion in his company and consequently was overwhelmed with panic at the thought of not being adequate to handle the demands of the job. During one session he said to me, "I'm a fake! Don't they know that I don't have a clue about what I'm doing?" His low self-confidence began to undermine him in ways that he wasn't even aware of. First, he began forgetting meetings, showing up unprepared, or arriving embarrassingly late. Then, he would be suddenly harsh with his staff and the next moment inappropriately solicitous. Eventually, his boss began to notice and tried to counsel him, but that only panicked him more. The problems continued. By the time he sought coaching, he had been fired from the job.

I'm Worried That I Can't Cut It Anymore

A crisis of self-confidence generally is accompanied by feelings of performance anxiety, and sometimes, even panic. The feelings become heightened when the executive finds himself in a situation that is unfamiliar, such as a new job, or when powerful others are depending on his performance. His own deeply held belief is that he doesn't have talent or ability to be in the position where he is and that he has made it this far because he is a fraud or his superiors have made a serious mistake. Consequently, the executive becomes increasingly anxious over his ability to handle his job.

Because this executive doesn't believe in his own ability, he has an exceptionally low tolerance for even the slightest criticism from others. He overreacts to such criticism, causing others to distance themselves from him.

CASE STUDY

A TOXIC REACTION

Sarah, a marketing executive at a trendy clothing manufacturer, came up with what she thought was a brilliant idea for a new advertising campaign. She mentioned her idea to a few friends and they loved it, so she decided to pitch it at the next marketing meeting. Sarah was always very careful before she pitched ideas. Other marketing executives would often throw out whatever ideas hit them in the moment, but not Sarah. She'd always worried that her peers might think her ideas were stupid. When the time came during the meeting to pitch the idea, Sarah began giving a short but well-rehearsed summary of the idea when, in the back of the room, peals of laughter rolled out. She was unnerved and became completely self-conscious to the point of forgetting the main theme of her idea. She quickly wrapped up her pitch and sat down, kicking herself for having thought the idea was good in the first place. The meeting moved on and another idea was adopted for the campaign. Later, after the meeting was finished, Sarah learned that the laughter that had erupted had nothing to do with her idea—apparently someone had cracked an unrelated joke in the back of the room.

The mortification, anger, and self-flagellation that well up inside an executive when he feels that he has somehow revealed his imagined incompetence is a toxic reaction that often causes him to act inappropriately. Other people are taken aback by his overreaction, which only makes him feel worse about himself. This sequence of events is so painful to him that he soon learns to avoid situations where he isn't completely confident of the outcome. This leads to a dramatic avoidance of change and a preoccupation with controlling any situation (e.g., presentations, performance appraisals, interviews) where his ability is on the line.

Self-Fulfilling Prophecy

Feelings of low self-confidence often become a self-fulfilling prophecy that causes the executive to perform poorly. Consider what happened to one client who later sought coaching.

C A S E
S T U D Y

AVOIDING DIFFICULT TRUTHS

Sam, the auditor, worked for an independent accounting firm. His job was, among many things, to meet with the CEO after the audit was complete and review the findings. At the end of one such engagement, Sam needed to tell the CEO some very unpleasant news. Fearing that the CEO might not accept the news and instead question the competence of his accounting firm, Sam stuttered and stammered as he tried to communicate the bad news. He was only able to spit out a small portion of the problem. Later, Sam compiled the audit report in which he explained the problem in detail, since he wasn't able to do in person. When the CEO read the report, he was furious and accused Sam of withholding critical information. The CEO felt blindsided by Sam not telling him the full story and subsequently fired the auditing firm.

As was the case with Sam, a crisis of self-confidence undermines the executive's true abilities and creates situations that confirm the executive's self-doubts. The cycle, if it persists, can continue until the executive starts to fail at the simplest of tasks.

One executive, caught in the grip of such a crisis, became so doubtful of his abilities that he could no longer write a straightforward memo. Trying to cover himself completely, he would ramble on about the issues until the real point he wanted to communicate was completely buried in a morass of extraneous details.

The Haves vs. the Have-Nots

An executive with a crisis of self-confidence often develops a resentment of other executives who appear confident and powerful. Threatened by their moxie, he will avoid dealing with them if possible. When he must deal with a confident executive, the relationship quickly takes an adversarial tone with every action of the confident executive construed as aggressive and even combative. The executive who has a crisis of self-confidence adopts a defensive attitude that sometimes includes silent sabotage of the confident executive.

One executive with a crisis of self-confidence actually wrote an anonymous memo to the entire group of senior executives and the CEO outlining a rival executive's illicit affair with an employee. Of course, the memo caused quite a stir and everyone was curious about, among many things, who wrote the memo. Unbeknownst to the memo writer, his computer used a particular font that wasn't readily available on other computers in the company. When the truth came to light, both executives were eventually asked to resign from the company.

It's Never Enough

The executive with a crisis of self-confidence may often achieve great success, but it is never enough. He will always point to the one thing that wasn't done perfectly, or that he didn't achieve the entire goal. Moreover, the executive may attribute his success to forces outside himself, such as luck or a strong economic environment, allowing himself to cling to his belief that his abilities are lacking.

CASE STUDY

WHEN SELF-DOUBT LINGERS

Nicole is the head of a medium-size consulting firm that has been, by all standards, very successful. A millionaire many times over, Nicole was depressed and unhappy about the business. She had a vague feeling that something was wrong, but couldn't identify what it was. She rode hard on the consultants who worked for her, pushing them to do more with less, but still the feeling that something was wrong remained. During coaching, the reason for her feeling became quite clear. Nicole was the daughter of a well-respected New England family who had wanted her to marry well and raise a family. Nicole had done neither, choosing instead to start her own business. She realized that she had internalized her parents' view of herself and had always doubted her ability to succeed as a businesswoman. No matter how much success she attained, the feeling lingered. Despite loads of evidence to the contrary, Nicole still doubted her ability to succeed.

Joy Busters

Some executives, especially those raised in deeply religious homes, have been taught since childhood that feelings of joy and pride are dangerous and should be avoided. When caught in a crisis of self-confidence, these executives will unconsciously bear an enormous burden of guilt for success. Who are they to enjoy so much success? This kind of executive will sometimes abandon a project at the height of its success just to avoid the guilt.

C A S E
S T U D Y

I DON'T DESERVE IT

Donald was an executive with a regional oil company who headed a project of buying automobile gas stations throughout the region. Over a decade, the company had amassed quite a profitable portfolio of over a hundred stations. In a move that surprised many within the company, Donald convinced the CEO to sell the profitable stations and invest in an experimental plant that produced road-paving materials from petroleum by-products. The CEO took Donald's advice, sold off all the stations, and invested in the plant. Within two years the plant was bankrupt and the company lost more than $30 million, not including all their losses resulting from the sale of the gas stations.

In coaching, Donald often spoke of his strict Catholic upbringing and his guilt over having such a lucrative salary compared to his siblings, one of whom was a priest and owned nothing. He felt that somehow he should be doing something more noble than making money. As we explored his feelings, it became apparent to Donald that his guilt had played a big role in the demise of his career and his imprudent decisions.

Although Donald had been highly successful early in his career, he had never really enjoyed that success. He rarely took vacations and often worried that "the higher I climb, the harder I'll fall." He said that he always knew the success would crumble—the only question for him was "when?" In many ways, he admitted, the downturn in his career was a relief.

The Fear Complex

The crisis of confidence is based on a fear complex of failure. Confidence begins to erode the greater the fear becomes; and the less confidence one has in oneself, the greater the fear of failure becomes. It's a hopeless and helpless trap that can be difficult to pull out of.

The basis of this fear complex is the belief that worth is defined by success. Without getting philosophical here, it is important that a person's sense of self-worth be based on his innate value as a living human being, not on what he accomplishes.

Why is this? Because the ego boost provided by accomplishments is only temporary. It gives a charge to the self-confidence and then fades. The next time a boost is needed, it must be a greater accomplishment. When an executive bases his sense of worth on how successful he is, he will ultimately never feel truly worthwhile.

For example, when I published my first book I felt I had completed a truly worthwhile and valuable accomplishment. A year later, however, after attending a writing conference and hearing a speaker say that you're not a successful writer until you've been published twice, I began to question my accomplishment. Not long after that, I realized that publishing could become a slippery slope for my self-confidence if I allowed it to. Once I'd published two books, then I would have my eye on making the best-seller list. On and on it would go, with my self-confidence slipping all the while.

Everyone fails at something. Everyone fails in some way every day. It's part of being human. When an executive tells himself that he cannot fail, and that if he does, he is somehow deficient, he sets himself up for certain failure. Throughout history, executives have failed miserably many times. The key isn't to fear failure, it's learning how to clean up your own messes!

Understanding the Life Script

The life script that most likely produces a crisis of confidence is a script that has carefully avoided situations that fully stretch the abilities of the executive. He doesn't test himself and therefore doesn't know either the extent of his strengths or his weaknesses. He imagines there are certain things he can't do, and he therefore avoids anything where he might fail.

An executive I once coached told me the story of how he had been keenly interested in going to medical school, but he didn't for fear that he couldn't make the grades required to graduate. Instead, he opted to take courses he felt more comfortable with and ultimately found himself attending business school.

What was tragic about his story is that he was a high-ranking executive for a pharmaceutical company. Although he wasn't a doctor, he had a brilliant mind and probably knew more about drugs in the human body than most doctors. There is no doubt that he would have done very well in medical school had he allowed himself to apply and attend. Much of his life he had accepted second- and third-best when he could have easily had the life he wanted if only he hadn't placed limits on himself.

This kind of life script is often set in motion by a strong Parent who continually warns the Child of the possible pitfalls that he might encounter. As a result, he becomes so focused on the possibilities for failure that his goal becomes one of minimizing those possibilities rather than choosing to do what makes him happy and fulfilled.

Finding the Courage

The key to inspiring courage within this executive to overcome his fear is to get him into action. The truth is, everyone experiences fear, but not everyone allows that fear to govern his life. Presidents giving speeches to the nation, teachers taking competency tests, and CEOs making presentations to employees all report feeling fear. What's important isn't that they feel the fear of failure, it's that they push through it and do what they have to do anyway. They refuse to allow the fear to control their lives.

By getting into action, the executive will begin to test his limits. This step almost always has the effect of building confidence, not destroying it.

Even executives who have failed grandly, and lost it all as a result, often report feeling empowered by the experience of getting into action. Why? Because it gave them a sense of how much power they really had. Sure, they may have made some mistakes, but they never knew how much they could actually accomplish. They realized that failure wasn't the end of the world, and they were able to get new jobs and still have stimulating careers. Until those limits are tested, the executive will continue to be caught in a fear complex of failure.

Confronting the Parent/Child Messages

There are two internalized childhood messages at the heart of the crisis of self-confidence that are worth understanding.

I'M NOT PARTICULARLY TALENTED AT ANYTHING

When an executive isn't aware of his talents, or believes he has no talent, his self-confidence is at risk. The executive whose career has been determined by others, and who has spent his time jumping from one job to the other or one department to another, may begin to feel that he has no particular talent. Since he hasn't had time to stay long enough with a job to see the rewards of his actions, he doesn't have any feedback on what it is that he does best.

It is critical to an executive's self-confidence that he knows exactly what it is that he has to offer the company. Until he knows that, he puts himself in situations where he isn't certain that he can succeed.

There are a number of ways for an executive to explore his talents. A good place to start is with talent inventories or 360-degree surveys. While none of these techniques is foolproof, they can provide some excellent information to the executive on what it is that he truly does well.

I'VE BECOME OBSOLETE

Sometimes an older executive who is increasingly surrounded by younger executives begins to feel that he is behind the times and obsolete. As a result, he may alter his behavior, allowing the younger executives to take on the technology issues or other work that he feels particularly ill-equipped to deal with.

The truth is that becoming obsolete only happens when you believe you are obsolete. No matter what your age, you engage in the practice of lifelong learning. You continually retool yourself by attending professional conferences or night classes, taking on new and different projects, and so on. It's only when you believe that you are obsolete that you stop doing these things.

213

Very often an executive convinces himself that he is out of date as a way to dodge the hard work involved in staying current. It isn't easy for anyone to stay current, young or old. The fact that an older executive has a complex frame of reference for the field in which he works is what gives him an advantage over younger workers. The older worker has a sense of history, what's worked and what hasn't, while younger workers are game for the latest fad that comes across the transom.

The real issue with an older executive isn't his age—it's why he wants to be obsolete. As long as he's willing to be curious and learn, he doesn't have to become any more out of date than his younger counterparts.

PART FIVE

TOOLS OF THE TRADE

This section of the book is a reference source for the executive coach. While earlier chapters dealt with identifying executives who might benefit from coaching (Chapter Four) or the covert ways executives avoid discomfort and get what they want (Chapter Eight), these last chapters provide tools the executive coach can use when beginning or building a coaching practice.

FIFTEEN

COACHING

TOOLS

This chapter describes various tools that can be helpful when coaching an executive. These tools can rejuvenate the process when the coaching sessions have reached a plateau. Sometimes, a simple activity, role-play, or questionnaire can bring up issues that are just beneath the surface.

A word of caution: Almost every novice coach relies too heavily on tools to keep the coaching sessions moving along. These tools should be used sparingly and never used as a substitute for client-directed coaching.

Coaching Plan

Below are the essential elements that are necessary for the coach to organize the information collected during coaching sessions and to bring focus to the work. Obviously, the coach's plan should never take precedence over the client's direction of the process. The plan is merely a tool for identifying issues and beginning the coaching process.

Coaching Plan

Client's Name:

Contact Information:

Fee Arrangement:

Initial Reason for Seeking Coaching:

Client's Crisis:

Underlying Fear Complex:

Triggering Events of Crisis:

Goals for Coaching:

Measures of Coaching Success:

Executive Crisis Questionnaire

Below is a questionnaire that can be helpful in identifying a client's crisis.

Please use the following scale to rate each statement to indicate how true each is of you:

1. Completely untrue of me.
2. Mostly untrue of me.
3. Slightly more true than untrue of me.
4. Moderately true of me.
5. Mostly true of me.
6. Describes me perfectly.

_____ 1. I turn to wiser or stronger people all the time for advice and guidance.

_____ 2. I avoid new challenges on my own.

_____ 3. I do not make my own decisions.

_____ 4. I do not enjoy being alone and avoid it if possible.

_____ 5. I often minimize my own needs, wants, and desires in an effort to please someone else.

_____ 6. I often feel that others are out to get what is rightfully mine.

_____ 7. I am reluctant to reveal my weaknesses because I expect that others will take advantage of them.

_____ 8. I am quick to attack others when I believe they will attack me.

_____ 9. I am often concerned that I will fail in a public situation (e.g., public speaking in an important meeting).

_____ 10. After the fact, I realize that I've sometimes been cruel or abusive to other people.

_____ 11. I don't tell others what I need from them and then am disappointed when my needs aren't met.

_____ 12. I often feel that others are not to be trusted.

_____ 13. Socializing with others is more of a chore than anything else.

_____ 14. Other people regularly disappoint me.

_____ 15. I'd enjoy my job if it weren't for the people I must work with.

_____ 16. My work is more drudgery than anything else.

_____ 17. Long ago, I gave up on realizing my dream.

_____ 18. I often think about doing something other than what I am doing now.

_____ 19. My life and career are driven mostly by obligation and responsibility.

_____ 20. I am not passionate about anything.

_____ 21. I have moved around a great deal in my career without really getting ahead.

_____ 22. I find myself in trouble if I stay in a job more than a few years.

_____ 23. I don't have a clear-cut profession or skill set.

_____ 24. I am more an "idea" person than a "mainte-nance" person.

_____ 25. I often start projects that I never complete.

_____ 26. I do not take the steps necessary to develop solid skills in my career (e.g., getting a graduate degree, reading the latest developments in professional journals, seeking out a mentor). I often try to coast and fool people about my expertise.

_____ 27. I chose a career below my potential.

_____ 28. I avoid taking the necessary steps to get promotions in my career (e.g., I do not promote myself, I stay in a dead-end job, or fail to ask/apply for a promotion).

_____ 29. I feel that I am basically untalented, and therefore feel fraudulent, even though objectively I have been quite successful.

_____ 30. I try to compensate for my lack of confidence by focusing on other assets (e.g., looks, charm, youthfulness), but underneath I still feel like a failure.

Scoring

Please add the item numbers, as indicated, for a total score for each crisis and then place the totals in the appropriate spaces.

Total Rating	Item Numbers	Crisis
	1-5	Individuation
	6-10	Inferiority
	11-15	Isolation
	16-20	Passion
	21-25	Commitment
	26-30	Self-Confidence

Satisfaction Graph

The satisfaction graph is a useful tool for helping a client identify (1) what's most important in his life and (2) where he isn't getting his needs met. It is a simple tool that requires the client to construct a graph that measures his experience of satisfaction in life. The real value of this tool is that once it's on paper you have the visual experience of the graph, which can often trigger insights that wouldn't occur otherwise.

The satisfaction graph is completed by having the client list the five or six things that are most important in his life. Examples might include his relationship with his spouse, time with his children, his financial security, his career advancement, and so on. It's strongly suggested that you not provide your client with examples unless he is unable to come up with meaningful areas on his own. Even the most benign example can influence your client's list. A big part of this exercise is encouraging the client to identify what's important to him (not what should be important).

Once the client has listed these areas, have him write them along the horizontal axis of a graph (see Figure 15-1).

Figure 15-1. Blank satisfaction graph.

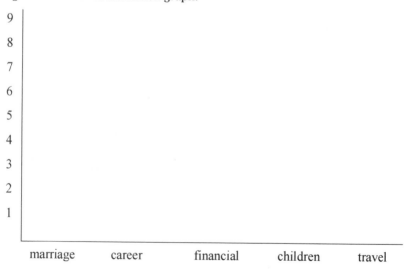

Once the client has done this, have him rate his satisfaction with each area of his life by placing a dot on the graph next to the corresponding number (higher numbers indicate more satisfaction). Then, ask the client to connect the dots with a line (see Figure 15-2).

Figure 15-2. Satisfaction graph.

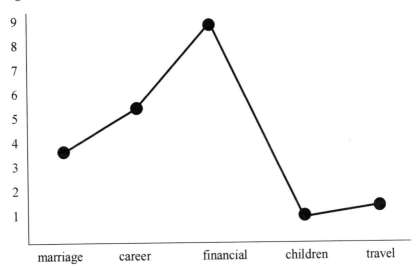

Once the graph is completed, have your client verbally explain the graph and each of the points on it. Sometimes this works well as a homework exercise that the client brings to following session and discusses.

The satisfaction graph is simple and easily completed. The result of using this tool is often a profound insight about one's life and aspirations. Seeing this information written on a paper in a familiar format often allows the client to view his life differently. The information in the graph can provide discussion material for several coaching sessions and may identify problem areas that the client was previously unable to discuss.

It may be helpful for the client to understand that the points on the graph are all related because one low point can anchor down the remainder of the graph. In other words, excessive dissatisfaction in one important area of your life can diminish the satisfaction you feel in all other areas. Likewise, when one low point is changed and satisfaction is increased, it often creates a momentum that increases satisfaction in all other areas as well.

Purpose Matrix

The purpose matrix (see Figure 15-3) is a good exercise for helping a client to focus on his life priorities. The various components of the matrix encourage the client to consider certain priorities that may have been neglected but are nonetheless important to him. This activity makes a great homework assignment for discussion at the following session.

Figure 15-3. Purpose matrix.

Dimension	Purpose
Professional	"To be promoted into an executive vice president position within five years"
Financial	"To invest/save enough to retire by 57 years old . . ."
Interpersonal	"To 'reignite' the romance with my wife"
Intellectual	"To read more and watch television less in the evenings"
Civic	"To be more involved with my son's Boy Scout troop"
Humanitarian	"To identify a charity that is meaningful to me and contribute both money and time"
Emotional	"To show my children that I love them more often"
Spiritual	"To find a church that inspires me more than my current affiliation"

Guided Imagery

Guided imagery can be a powerful way of eliciting feelings from the client. There are many scenarios that may be used, but here are just a few to give you an idea. In reality, you'll want to create a guided imagery that's appropriate for the client's particular issues.

DEATHBED SCENE

Imagine yourself very old and on your deathbed. Your life is passing before you. Close your eyes. Watch your life as it passes, scene by scene, up to the present moment.

❖ What memories bring you the most pain? The most joy?

❖ What experiences, commitments, and accomplishments have given meaning to your life?

❖ Do you have any regrets? If so, what could you have done differently? What can you do differently now?

❖ Were there choices you made that you weren't aware of at the time?

❖ What fears affected your life? How did you handle them? How can you handle them differently now?

❖ Did you discover anything of great value? What are your values?

❖ Did you discover something you want to change now?

ONE YEAR LEFT

Imagine that you have one year left to live. You can spend that year with whomever you wish, doing whatever you want.

❖ Whom would you choose to have with you during that year? Does this person know that you feel this way now?

❖ How will you spend your time?

❖ Is there anything you want to accomplish during this year?

❖ What will you choose not to do during this year? Why?

NEWSPAPER STORY

Image that you wake up one morning and at the breakfast table you read the newspaper as you always do. Suddenly you realize that the front-page headline and story is about you.

❖ What does the headline say?

❖ How are you described in the story?

❖ What is the "hook" in the story of your life that makes it a front-page story?

❖ What elements of the story would you change if you could?

❖ What is the climax of the story? What is the climax you want the story to have?

❖ How does the story end?

❖ Is this a story that others want to read?

"I" STATEMENTS

"I" statements are a common technique used among psychotherapists to encourage their clients to take responsibility for their own behavior. The chart in Figure 15-4 lists several statements that clients sometimes make and also lists ways to help the client restructure the statements as "I" statements. Each client's issues are different, so you'll want to work with the client to restructure his own statements of blame and external attribution (being controlled by something other than his own free will).

Activating

Activating is another technique that helps the client take responsibility for his own actions (see Figure 15-5). It is very similar to the "I" statement exercise since it requires the client to rephrase issues in a way that demonstrates his control over what

Figure 15-4. "I" statements.

Client Statement	"I" Statement
"I can't."	I choose not to," or "I won't."
"You didn't tell me."	"That's not what I heard."
"He made me do it."	"I reacted to him."
"That guy drives me up the wall."	"I allow him to anger me."
"This situation is driving me crazy."	"I am continually worrying about this situation."
"My job is stressful."	"I stress over my job."
"You don't give me any choice."	"I have decided to take this action."
"Working here is making me ill."	"I'm not handling working here very well."

Figure 15-5. Activation statements.

Client Statement	Activation
"I am depressed."	"I am depressing (myself)."
"I am angry."	"I am 'angering.'"
"I am stressed out."	"I am stressing myself out."
"My life is a mess."	"I am messing up my life."
"I am trapped in this job."	"I am trapping myself in this job."
"I am bored."	"I am boring myself."

is happening. The technique involves having the client add "-ing" to descriptive phrases he uses about himself. Although this exercise often creates nonexistent words, the effect is to underline the active role of the client in creating the situation.

Metaphor Map

In this activity, you ask the client to think of a metaphor that aptly describes how he feels about his life, career, relationships, or whatever the particular issue at hand is and then draw it in a picture. For example, one executive drew a picture of a space alien sitting in a corporate office and described himself as feeling completely out of place and alien to his job. Another executive drew a picture of a man bailing water out of a sinking boat. The caption above the man read: "I'm bailing as fast as I can." This executive saw his career as a sinking ship that he was frantically, and not so successfully, trying to rescue. Finally, the map in Figure 15-6 illustrates how one executive felt that the pressures of his job held him in an excruciating vise.

Figure 15-6. Metaphor map example.

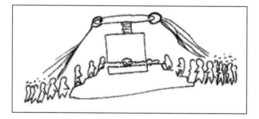

©2001 Annette Simmons. For more information on metaphor maps please visit *www.groupprocessconsulting.com*.

Role-Playing

The last tool we'll discuss is role-playing. While this familiar tool is used in many contexts, it can be especially valuable at certain points in the coaching process. There are two primary forms of role-playing. One form is where the executive plays himself and the coach plays another person, a devil's advocate, the boss, for example. Another very effective form of this tool is to reverse it and have the coach play the role of the executive and the executive play the role of the other person. This reverse form of role-playing can "loosen" the client's hold on his own perception of the circumstance and help him begin to understand and empathize with other people's perspectives.

When working with the three ego states, it can be very helpful to have the client role-play the conversation that might occur between two ego states, such as Parent and Child, or Child and Adult. When doing this type of role-playing, it is often helpful to use an empty chair to symbolize one of the ego states. For example, you tell the client to role-play the conversation between his internal Parent and Child with him playing the Parent speaking to the Child sitting in the empty chair. The empty chair is merely a prop, but it can be very effective in making real for the client the otherwise internal and abstract conversation.

SIXTEEN

THE BUSINESS

OF COACHING

For those starting a new executive coaching practice, there are several important issues to consider. Location, credentials, ethics, and billing practices can become important determinants of your success. In this chapter, we discuss some of these issues and recommend ways of handling them.

Location, Location, Location

One of the most important issues for the beginning coach is where to locate. Ideally, a coach is located in a metropolitan area where there is easy access to many of the larger corporations. While it isn't absolutely necessary to be in the same city as your clients, you will find it a great help in building your practice. It is extremely difficult for a beginning coach to build a practice long distance.

Shortly after starting my coaching practice, I moved to Key West, Florida for personal reasons. If you've ever visited Key West, you know it is fairly remote and certainly no center of corporate business. Luckily, I had a number of clients before I moved, but I found myself working extra long hours, many of which weren't paid for, just to keep the same level of effectiveness with my clients. While I did find coaching over the phone helpful, it was clearly no substitute for face-to-face sessions. As a result, I often found myself flying to the client's location. The time and cost involved made long-distance coaching very difficult.

Another important downside to long-distance coaching is that you eliminate a large number of potential clients who will see you only if they can easily get to your office. For many reasons, clients would rather come to your office than have you visit them. Hiring a coach in another city is just too great a barrier, so they either find one who is local or go without coaching.

If you are not located in a regional business center (e.g., Seattle, Atlanta, Houston, New York), you might consider making a move before trying to start a new coaching practice. To maximize your chances of success, you're much better off if you start in an area that has a large number of potential clients.

Starting a Coaching Practice

One of the most important aspects to building a coaching practice is trustworthiness and professionalism. Executives who are in crisis need someone in whom they can confide their most protected secrets, and they'll only do so with someone they trust.

Creating an environment that is conducive to trust has many components, but it includes having a professional office space, solid credentials (e.g., an advanced degree in business,

232

organizational behavior, or psychology), and plenty of experience working as an executive.

The question is often asked about what kind of advanced degree is best for the executive coach. Should the coach be a trained psychologist, psychotherapist, or MBA graduate? My experience has been that the answer is all of the above. Those who have attempted to become coaches with only a psychology background have difficulty relating to the world of the executive. Likewise, the MBA graduate is often too bottom line–oriented to do the sometimes-ambiguous work of coaching. Successful coaches almost always have a combination of credentials. They are psychologists who have significant experience as business executives, or former executives who have returned to graduate school to study psychology or counseling. Since executive coaching is a new field and doesn't squarely fit within the current academic models (with their traditionally drawn distinctions between the social sciences and business curriculum) the executive coach must design his own training.

In addition, it is very helpful to attend one of several high-quality certificate programs that grant executive coach certifications. Two of these programs include:

1. *Center for Executive Coaching* at the Professional School of Psychology, 425 University Avenue, Suite 201, Sacramento, CA 95825. The Professional School of Psychology is an accredited institution that offers graduate degrees in all areas of psychology.

2. *CoachU*, P.O. Box 25117, Colorado Springs, Colorado 80936-5117. CoachU is an organization that is specifically focused on the training, certification, and continuing education of executive coaches.

Once you have those baseline criteria met, you must allow yourself a minimum of a year to begin to build a coaching practice. A coaching practice is not something that is built overnight or even in a few months. It takes time for your reputation to grow and for referrals to begin expanding your business.

It's been my experience, and the experience of coaches with whom I've worked, that the best marketing is from word of mouth. Coaching is highly personal, and an executive will trust the recommendation of a good friend or colleague over any brochure or speech that you might give. Unfortunately, word-of-mouth referrals take a good deal of time to develop, so be prepared to give your practice the time it needs to grow. Most coaches don't begin to make a profit from their work until they've been coaching for two or more years.

Structuring the Sessions

I've experimented with dozens of arrangements with my clients, but I continually find myself coming back to the one-hour-per-week session. It's difficult to do quality coaching for more than an hour, and the client needs the week between sessions to absorb and think about what happened. Only in times of acute crisis is more frequent coaching effective.

During your first meeting with the client, it's important to set the stage for your work together. It's been my experience that it takes at least ten sessions for the work to begin to see results, so I generally require the client to agree to attend a minimum of twelve sessions before deciding whether to continue the coaching. If coaching is going to be effective, it almost always is by the twelfth session.

Pricing Your Services

Coaching prices can vary significantly within each region of the country, but as a general rule, coaching services are offered between $100–$300 per session (including lengthy telephone calls when coaching is included). Some experienced, high-level coaches charge as much as $1,000 a session, but this is rare and then only happens with the most senior executives of large corporations. Clients are always billed for missed sessions, just as if they had attended. A significant part of establishing your professionalism is in your fee and your expectation that the client pay his bill in a timely manner. You should always be direct and clear about payment for your services.

This brings us to some of the most common dilemmas a coach encounters. If the company pays for your services, does it have a right to know what is discussed in your sessions? Can the company prevent the coach from recommending the client quit his job? Should the company have some measurable objective of the success of coaching? In short, if the company pays the bill, does it get some control over what happens?

Broadly speaking, yes, the company should see some ultimate success from coaching. But remember, one of the secrets to successful coaching is that the client does the work and, consequently, controls the sessions. It is up to the client, not the company or the coach, to ensure that benefit is derived from coaching. In terms of specific information from a coaching session, the coach should never reveal that, regardless of who pays for the services.

The company that hires an executive coach to work with executives must clearly understand that a possible outcome of the coaching may be that the executive leaves the company. The point is this: If the executive ultimately chooses to leave the company, it is probably best for the executive and the company in the long run. If an executive isn't fulfilled in the job, then he isn't motivated to give his best to the company. In this case, all parties are served well when the executive moves on to other opportunities.

Confidentiality

Everything discussed in a coaching session should be held with the strictest confidentiality. Even when the company is paying for the coaching services, all coaching information should remain confidential. It's important for the effectiveness of coaching that your client knows that this is your practice from the very first session.

In some rare cases, an internal employee can do executive coaching as long as the coach and the coach's superiors honor the confidentiality rule. It's usually a mistake to house a coach in the human resources department, since many executives will assume that what is discussed will be used in making employment decisions. Furthermore, the internal coach should be shielded from organizational politics and power games. If the coach is concerned about his own career, he may be less likely to confront a powerful executive who could affect his employment.

Ethics

The field of executive coaching is still emerging from the traditional disciplines of psychology and business management. Since it is evolving, there is no universally accepted code of ethics. The following is a good example of a pledge of ethics that is used by CoachU, an organization that offers training in executive coaching:

CoachU Standards & Ethics [1]

I . CLIENT AND COACH RELATIONSHIP

As a coach, I pledge to honor and support the beliefs, values, individuality, objectives, and goals of my client(s) so that they can grow and expand the areas of their personal and/or professional lives that they have chosen. In doing so I pledge to respect my clients' individual requirements, limitations, and personal boundaries. I will remain constructive and instrumental in any feedback or exchange between us and will put first and only the well-being and expressed desires of my client(s) and at no time my own self-interest or personal gain as it pertains to the coach/client relationship.

II. CONFIDENTIALITY

I agree to maintain the confidentiality of my client(s) and the coaching relationship. I will hold confidential the name(s) of my client(s), information about their personal and/or professional life, colleagues, or related parties without the express permission from the client.

III. PROFESSIONAL CONDUCT

I will provide coaching to clients only in the areas of my expertise. I will not offer guidance, advice, or council in any specialized area in which I am not qualified or licensed. If it becomes apparent that the client has challenges or problems that are beyond my expertise, I will request that clients seek advice, counsel, or services from a qualified professional to help them in that area. I will reserve the right to terminate the relationship until the client has done so if the challenge or problem impedes the forward movement of the coaching process.

IV. PROFESSIONAL DEVELOPMENT

I pledge to continually pursue my development as a professional coach by making a commitment to my own personal growth and exploration, maintaining a connection to the coaching community at large by meeting regularly (a minimum of once bimonthly) in either a live or virtual group of peers, professional coaching organization(s), or coach training organization(s), and participating in a minimum of ten hours of coaching-related classes, workshops, seminars, conferences, or conventions per year.

A Final Word

The field of executive coaching is young and evolving. As the field matures and the business environment changes, undoubtedly the issues related to the business of coaching will change, too. One thing, however, must never change. If the field is to survive and coaches are to remain successful, we must be steadfastly focused on the unique service we provide.

We are not management consultants. We are not "shadow executives" used to prop up other poorly performing executives. We are not time-management specialists.

We are experts in two of the most critical elements of the successful executive: strong motivation to get the job done and the ability to build solid business relationships. As coaches, we help our clients reach their highest potential in both of these areas. It is the expertise of the coach in helping the client resolve his internal conflicts and crises that propels the field forward and that makes executive coaches an essential part of achieving the best possible business results.

Note

1. Copyright 2000, CoachU, P.O. Box 25117, Colorado Springs, Colorado 80936-5117, U.S.A.; reprinted with permission.

INDEX